Feel
the
Vibes

How to be a Successful Psychic

First published by O Books, 2008
O Books is an imprint of John Hunt Publishing Ltd., The Bothy, Deershot Lodge, Park Lane, Ropley,
Hants, SO24 0BE, UK
office1@o-books.net
www.o-books.net

Distribution in:	South Africa
	Alternative Books
UK and Europe	altbook@peterhyde.co.za
Orca Book Services	Tel: 021 555 4027 Fax: 021 447 1430
orders@orcabookservices.co.uk	
Tel: 01202 665432 Fax: 01202 666219	Text copyright Joanne Brocas 2008
Int. code (44)	
	Design: Stuart Davies
USA and Canada	
NBN	ISBN: 978 1 84694 153 5
custserv@nbnbooks.com	
Tel: 1 800 462 6420 Fax: 1 800 338 4550	All rights reserved. Except for brief quotations
	in critical articles or reviews, no part of this
Australia and New Zealand	book may be reproduced in any manner without
Brumby Books	prior written permission from the publishers.
sales@brumbybooks.com.au	
Tel: 61 3 9761 5535 Fax: 61 3 9761 7095	The rights of Joanne Brocas as author have
	been asserted in accordance with the
Far East (offices in Singapore, Thailand,	Copyright, Designs and Patents Act 1988.
Hong Kong, Taiwan)	
Pansing Distribution Pte Ltd	
kemal@pansing.com	A CIP catalogue record for this book is available
Tel: 65 6319 9939 Fax: 65 6462 5761	from the British Library.

Printed by Digital Book Print

Feel
the
Vibes

How to be a Successful Psychic

Joanne Brocas

BOOKS

Winchester, UK
Washington, USA

CONTENTS

DEDICATION AND ACKNOWLEDGMENTS

I dedicate this book to my soul mate and husband Jock Brocas.
Jock is a constant in my life and his ambition inspires me, he
encourages me to always reach for my highest potential.

I cannot fail to mention an important dedication to my spiritual
teachers, for without their guidance and teachings this book
would not exist.

To Gillian Sharpe, President of Oxford Street Christian
Spiritualist Church and truly the best medium I have ever
known.

To Linda Paterson, who gave me my first ever message from
spirit bringing through my Grandmother and opening my eyes
to the sixth sense.

Finally to my Grandmother in spirit Gladys Joce, I know with
my heart and soul that she helps to guide and heal me along my
life's path.

Foreword

By Jessica Adams, psychic astrologer for international editions of Vogue and Cosmopolitan.

If you think you might be a born psychic or medium, this book will save you a lot of time. Joanne Brocas is not only one of the most accurate readers I have ever come across, she also gives friendly, warm, down-to-earth advice about managing the sixth sense.

At eight years old, she was having premonitions about finding spiders in her orange juice in the fridge! At 21 she was a hard-working hairdresser in Wales. Today Joanne has a popular website and long waiting list of clients from all over the world. Along the way, she has learned real-world techniques for seeing the future, communicating with spirit people and manifesting your dreams. This book generously brings those real-world techniques to you.

Have you ever wondered why you are sensitive to noise, or why you cannot bear negative news or violence on television? Joanne has good advice on this, and other signs of psychic ability. Have you ever long to feel the vibes about a new man on a first date? There is good advice on this too. You may also be intrigued by special methods to check out insurance salesmen, used car salesmen, and even your choice of holiday this summer. In this way, you will soon get your psychic abilities flowing.

The world of life after death can be confusing and even frightening without a sensible guide. That is another reason why you may find this book useful. As a medium, Joanne has dealt with murder investigations and missing person cases. She is also familiar with psychic attack and the dark side. In this book you will find out practical ways to deal with it all.

If you are already on the path of psychic work or mediumship, or you are excited about the possibility that you might be gifted in this way, then Feel the Vibes is an excellent addition to your bookshelf. Reading Joanne's words is like listening to a trusted girlfriend. Start reading right here and your future could start to look really interesting!

Jessica Adams

Introduction

You are already psychic. Everyone on this planet is born with a sixth sense and this natural psychic ability can be developed and fine tuned to a successful level, leading to becoming a successful psychic. *Feel the Vibes* is a book that will show you how to strengthen your inner power and use your vibes to enhance your life and gain a spiritual understanding of life and death. It will explain how you can use your vibes to read the energy around people, places and objects as well as looking into the past, present and future, giving accurate psychic readings.

You will be filled with an understanding of how your vibes attract certain people and situations into your life and ways in which to use your vibes to create what you desire. This book will also show you how to protect yourself from negative influences like earthbound spirits and what is known as psychic attack. You will learn about evil and its influences as well as the power of the light. I will show you how to open up to the spirit world in a controlled and safe manner to be able to receive messages and speak to loved ones who have crossed over. I also explain the difference between psychics and mediums and the benefits of their roles.

You already use your psychic senses daily – most of the time this is done unconsciously. As you are already psychic, I do not teach you anything new, I just help you to develop what is already within you. The psychic exercises and information in this book will help you to unlock the hidden senses and bring them to the surface to be fine tuned. The more you practice anything in life, the stronger and more confident you become. This confidence will help you to use your vibes and give you the ability to tune into energy accurately.

The word psychic comes from the Greek word 'Psyche' meaning soul – the creative and divine part of you that is connected to God. You are filled with this wonderful divine spark and have this power to use, to create the world around you. There are guides and angels assigned to each one of you helping you to fulfil your destiny and to keep you safe until it is your time to pass. This book will show you how to connect to your spiritual helpers that will serve you well in your psychic development.

You will be able to use your psychic ability in the present moment to help you solve your problems and to make constructive life choices to bring about a happier future. I will show you how you can do this for others if it is your desire to become a professional psychic reader. Your vibes have brought you to purchase this book and you have now made the wise decision to start your psychic journey. A journey that can bring tremendous rewards, go through each chapter and contemplate the knowledge as well as using the psychic practices. You will develop at your own pace and put as much commitment in as you desire, remember the more commitment you give, the faster you develop and the stronger your vibes become. Each chapter will provide you with a deeper understanding of feeling the vibes, building in your development through to the very end. Good luck on your journey, you have just set in motion the beginning of becoming a successful psychic.

Joanne Brocas

CHAPTER ONE

Vibes and how they work

Are you ready to change your life? Do you feel inspired to discover the successful psychic within? You have the power and the spiritual gifts inside of you, to become a successful psychic for yourself and to others. To be able to reach this successful level, you need to understand what being psychic actually means and how a psychic works. We all have a sixth sense and intuition or gut instinct that gives us vibes about certain people, things, and situations. Vibes are energy vibrations that are a part of us and just like our physical skin covers our body, so do our vibes surround and cover us.

This is called our aura and everyone has one and so does inanimate objects or non living things. Our vibes can be described as our true inner feelings about the way we perceive ourselves, others and life itself. All knowledge about us is contained within our individual vibrations and psychics are able to interpret and read these vibes to obtain information. Our vibes contain the truth about our real feelings even though we may try to hide this from others; we cannot hide it within our vibes and aura.

People who put on masks for the outside world to hide their pain and pretend to be happy when they are not, will resonate at a state of unhappiness and express inner pain through their vibrations. This is going against the true joy of their spirit and so conflict between the mind and spirit emanates within their vibes. Their individual vibration reveals the truth of what they really feel and if ignored can end up causing physical or emotional problems with their health.

We are energy vibes in motion, meaning our vibes change when we experience different moods, thoughts and feelings. The vibes we express act like a magnetic pull to other vibes of the same vibration, and so this becomes our point of attraction, 'like attracts like'. Think right now, about where your thoughts and feelings are focussed, are they on a high and positive vibration or on a lower and negative vibration? Wherever your true feelings are, you are attracting more of the same vibrations to you, even when you pretend or mask them. An example of this, if someone has asked you if you felt ok and you answered yes, when in truth you really felt miserable and low, you would be hiding your true feelings with a false pretence. You would also be attracting more of those low feelings to you and you wonder why things are not improving. Remember, vibes are controlled by our true feelings and thoughts and attract this way, whether we are conscious of this or not.

Our Spiritual Essence

To gain a deeper understanding of feeling the vibes a psychic needs to know where their psychic senses come from. They do this by discovering more about the bigger picture of life through learning the truth of who they really are, where they came from and why they are here? Each one of us has a soul and our soul contains our spiritual essence or higher self, it is immortal and will exist for eternity, our spiritual blueprint of the Divine. Our physical body and aura is where the soul is housed for its journey and duration on Earth. Connecting our physical body to our aura is our etheric or energy body that surrounds and interpenetrates us and is a replica of our physical frame. Our etheric body has different levels of vibration known as subtle bodies extending outwards and this is what makes up the auric field. The etheric body is filled with universal life force energy and this energy enters us via chakras and is what sustains our physical body, enabling us to live life on earth. We hold inside of us our divine purpose and destiny and all that we need to know to complete our journey on Earth. There is one powerful source in this universe and that is the Divine Power of the Creator God. Our soul is a spark of this divine power because we are created in the image and likeness of God, and we use our soul power, to create our lives. Our soul power includes our psychic senses that enable us to use our vibes to make the best of our lives, assisting us in fulfilling our destiny.

Whenever we use our soul powers or tap into our energy source, we increase the amount of life force energy received and our vibes are raised. When we are filled with the stresses and strains of the material world we decrease the amount of life force energy within and we experience problems. Another way in which our life force energy is depleted is when our human ego or rational mind gets in the way of our spiritual nature and causes an imbalance. Material problems can weigh heavily on the ego mind and quickly lower our vibes.

A word of warning when developing the psychic senses, if you are emotionally unstable because of too many material problems, you need to wait until you are in a more balanced state of mind. This is because you are becoming more sensitive to the subtle vibrations around you and you risk being affected by these energies, they can leave you feeling drained and open to psychic attack if you are off balance. This will be explained in further detail in a later chapter.

To be able to find balance and quieten the ego mind you must be able to master or keep check of your emotions and face obstacles and problems from a stand point of, changing what needs to be changed and accepting what can not. Psychic development is about developing awareness and understanding of the real you, it gives you the platform to develop your intuition enabling you to listen to your soul. Acknowledge the fact that you are more than just a body with a mind and take full advantage of the fact that you are a brilliant creative soul.

The Mind – Body Connection

In developing the psychic senses it is helpful to learn more about the body, mind and spirit connection, the ego belongs to our human rational mind, our conscious awareness and level of learning and beliefs from our birth to the age we are now. Our ego has one job and that is to keep us safe from harm so it can survive. It does not recognize it has a soul and thinks that it must control the body in order to survive and live. If the ego thinks it may be under threats of any kind it will do what it can to get your attention. It does this by using fearful or limiting thoughts to influence the person and tries to gain control of the will or personality, which unbeknownst to the ego is also influenced by the soul. If we are unaware of our soul and our divine power to create our lives, we diminish the spiritual part of our selves and end up listening to the ego and living life with just the five senses. To live life by also listening to what the heart is feeling is one sure way to incorporate the language of the soul and initiate the power of the sixth sense.

By listening to our soul and to the intuition that we are born with, we can make wiser life choices without any limiting fears. This can quieten the ego and balance the mind, body and spirit connection. The rational mind will be scientific and only interested in seeing something, so to believe it, the soul knows different and helps the body rely on feelings to believe. We do still need the rational mind though, so we can think things through and make decisions to keep us safe. A successful psychic knows the importance of balancing the senses the goal is to use the common sense of the five senses along with using your vibes to create your world. Do not let your rational mind talk you out of, or stop you from developing your psychic side just because it has no scientific proof. To be open-minded is the first step to believing that you are more than just your mind with its ego and physical body. Open-mindedness is you expanding your conscious awareness to gain knowledge of the spiritual part of you and the universe in which you exist.

Balancing Our Vibes

Every one of us has a desire to be happy in life, to live life with ease and experience peace of mind. To achieve this happiness then we must come to realize that we have the power within us to create it ourselves. Your vibes will give you the gentle clues that help you to align with the pleasurable, joyful feeling that is your true nature. The key is to listen to how you are feeling in any given moment and choose the things that help you to feel good inside. By listening to the truth of your hearts desires, you are listening to your soul. When we balance the feelings that our heart and soul are expressing along with our five senses to create the best overall choice, we create a successful outcome. Using our vibes daily can help us to monitor these feelings thus controlling our level of attraction. I cannot imagine not using my vibes each day to check in with how things make me feel inside. By the time you have finished reading this book, you too will know the benefits of always checking in with your vibes and it will become second nature.

Material concerns can leave their mark on us and our feelings can alter rapidly because of this, lowering our vibes and point of attraction. Our five senses can help us to work things out rationally and our sixth sense can help us to listen to our wisdom within, taking the risks we need that will help us move on. If you love something with your heart and soul, then you can be sure you are listening to the voice of your spirit. Going against the true joy of your soul and doing things that you dislike or cannot even bear, will crush your spirit and lower your vibes. We need to be able to find ways in which to balance our psychic senses along with our five senses to live happily in the material world. We do this through spiritual awareness, exploring the notion that death is an illusion and life is eternal. There is no end to spiritual advancement and once one aspect has been understood a whole new world of questions opens up and the student becomes eager to learn as much as they can. Once you start the spiritual path, you will never go back, you will notice that the ego becomes less bothersome and so you balance the energies of Heaven and Earth. This helps us to live our truth and follow our heart always being true to ourselves. Balance is the key word here, as life on earth needs the five senses to survive, but without any spiritual knowledge of who you are, along with the use of your soul powers then life will not be complete or fulfilling. Spiritual development goes hand in hand in becoming a successful psychic enhancing the sixth sense.

Here is a quick example of being out of balance one way or the other. If someone is five sensory, ignoring their sixth sense and spiritual blueprint, then they will be totally focussed on the material world, making ends meet and following the routine of day to day life. They listen to their ego mind and let fearful thoughts keep them stuck in their life. They feel that there is something missing but cant quite put their finger on what it is, so they search for things to keep them satisfied. This satisfaction can be felt from many different sources like focussing on money, alcohol, drugs, food, sex but in extremes. I call this spiritually sleeping or not seeing the light, and boy can I tell when I meet a five sensory person. The way I tell is purely because of the way they make me feel as they are on a different vibration. I do not attract them into my life I only come across them and when I do, I marvel at how different our outlooks in life are. On the other hand a sixth sensory person who ignores their rational mind and the common sense of the fives senses are also off balance. These people make me laugh and I call them airy fairy folk, they are totally out of touch with reality and live by signs from anything to everything. I have literally come across people who will not buy toilet roll without first checking with their guide to see if it's the best colour. Now what guide in their right mind is bothered abut the colour of the toilet roll as we all know what's going to happen to that. Anyway airy fairy folk are those who have terrible problems with finances and at the same time are praying to their angels and guides to give them the lottery numbers by assuring them they will give some of the money to charity, thinking they can bargain their way with the spirit world. All of this is out of touch with reality, they need to ground and use their rational mind to assert themselves, if not they will just live in their imaginations and create the fantasy land to fit their needs. Remember a successful psychic is a balanced psychic.

Residual Energy

So now you know that you have an energy field of vibes called an aura. This aura gives out and receives energy vibrations and this is what a psychic uses to read their client or to feel the energy of a place or object. When we receive other people's energy, we feel their moods and emotions and this can have an effect on us. This is fine if the person is joyous and happy as it can leave us feeling up-lifted and happy too. The problem is when they are depressed and miserable, then we too can feel fed up, tired and over emotional. Most often or not we are unaware that we are picking up on other people's vibes and can wonder why, we feel so down when there are no reasons for us to feel that way. To be able to feel, understand and read energy, is what will make a psychic become accurate and successful in their psychic development. This is paramount to the unfolding of the psychic senses, also helping to fine tune your intuition to work for you, in your daily life. Ways in which we can feel energy vibes is through visiting places that contain strong residual energy or what is known as imprints from emotional situations and tragic events. One eerie place to experience these vibes is at Inverness in Scotland, where the great battle of Culloden happened in 1746. My husband and I often visit these places to be able sense the atmospheric changes and notice how it makes us feel. This is how we tune into and read the energy vibes of the place to receive information from the past. You may have noticed and felt this if you have visited any old castles or any other areas where emotional events occurred. We will go into more detail about residual energy and ghosts in a later chapter on ghosts and hauntings.

Psychometry and the Psychic Senses

We are now going to look at the ways in which a psychic works, in preparation for our first psychic practice of reading an item of jewellery. The reading of energy vibrations is called psychometry – psyche is the Greek word for soul, so psychometry is, reading the souls energy. The soul contains within, every record of all events ever experienced and felt, along with its complete knowledge and level of development since the time it became an individual spark of energy. Everything in the universe consists of energy and information, even non living things like a table and chair. The famous scientist Albert Einstein came to the startling conclusion that matter and energy were interrelated, what we see with our physical eyes such as an object, is just energy vibrating at a certain frequency, making it solid becoming matter. The reason we are able to read an object and gain information from it about the owner, is that their energy vibes will have been absorbed into the object and more so if it is a treasured item and worn often. Psychometry can be developed through practice and an understanding of how your vibes interpret the information received through the psychic senses. Psychics use psychometry to assist the police in missing persons cases or murder investigations, they can read photographs, tune into a crime scene by being in the place it happened or through a clue left there. My husband and I have worked on missing persons cases by receiving a photo of the person thus helping us to gain a psychic link and we were able to tell from this that the person would return home safe and well, which I am pleased to say they did. Anything can be used to read the vibes if they contain a person's energy, making it possible to establish a connection. Once a psychic has an energy link through psychometry, they can tap into the history of past events up to the present moment, as everything will be available to be read. The main psychic senses you will be using to receive information when reading energy include clairvoyance, clairaudience, clairsentience, as well as intuition and a claircognisance or what is known as, just knowing. I will explain this in greater detail as we move along. Other psychic senses that psychics and mediums use, are telepathy or what is known as a mind to mind connection, as well as smelling and tasting odours that are expressed through the vibes.

Everyone is Psychic

Just remember that everyone is psychic as everyone has a soul and with practice this natural psychic ability can be trained and developed. It is already within you so I am not teaching you anything you do not already posses. I am just giving you the spiritual knowledge and tools for you to understand how to use your natural given senses in a controlled and safe manner. Using the tools and psychic practices will strengthen your vibes increasing self-confidence, accuracy and fulfilment. The more you practice anything in life the stronger and more gifted you become. We will start by reading objects of jewellery as this is our grounding before we move into the more advanced psychic work of reading people, places and looking into the future and also using mediumship. Remember that we all give off energy vibrations or vibes as I call them and each person's energy is like a finger print with their own DNA. So you can receive very accurate information from using psychometry to read the vibes.

You are already using your psychic senses, sometimes without even being aware of it, like when the phone is ringing and you know who it is, before you answer it or when you walk into a room and you have a warm sensation or an uncomfortable one. This is you tapping into the vibes, energy of who is calling on the phone, or from the energy imprints left in the room. Other instances are when you may have been thinking of someone you haven't seen in a very long time and you end up bumping into them or they contact you from out of the blue. You may find that the other person had also been thinking of you and so both of your vibes have brought you together.

The first thing I teach my students is belief. If they choose to believe in the fact that they have a psychic ability already within them, then they are setting the positive intention of developing it. If they have no belief in themselves or the fact that they are 'surely not psychic' then this can affect their vibes and their psychic ability is temporarily blocked. You do not need to totally believe though, having an open mind is enough as long as you remain in a state of expectation and discovery and not one of defeatism before you even try. Now before we begin with reading an object, let's look into how you receive the information through your vibes. You have already mastered how to use your physical senses and I will show you how to master your psychic senses. This means you will be using the senses inside of yourself 'subjectively' through your inner vision called clairvoyance, inner hearing called clairaudience and inner feelings or sensing known as clairsentience. We also have intuitive flashes of inspiration that give us gut instincts about certain decisions and telepathic abilities or what can be called mind to mind connections and this is often dis-played with twins. One knows what the other one is thinking or feeling and can tell if something has happened when they are miles apart. Twins claim to be able to hold conversations by telepathic abilities and can answer each other by their thoughts alone.

The Three Minds
It is thought that the mind contains our conscious, subconscious and super-conscious awareness. The part of the mind that is used for telepathic or psychic work, are the subconscious and

super conscious minds. The first thing we are going to explore is discovering ways in which our vibes work via our dream state; here we can see how information is given in the forms of clues, symbolic and actual information. When we sleep at night our waking mind becomes still and our subconscious mind becomes alive and we are filled with memories of the day and other scenarios needing our attention. Our dream state can alert us through images and symbols what we need our emotional selves to deal with in waking reality. If we pay attention to our dreams we may find solutions to our problems in our waking life. It is wise to keep a journal at the side of the bed to record any dreams that are vivid or strong enough to leave its message in your conscious mind. To understand the language of the dream, first you need to take notice to what kind of dream you have had.

The Language of Dreams
Nightmares
Nightmares or dreams that cause you fear and anxiety are symbolic of situations that you cannot face in your waking reality. You may feel that someone is chasing you and trying to harm you in some way, leaving you feeling fearful and vulnerable. This can mean that at present in an area of your life's circumstances you are feeling vulnerable and fear the outcome of your situation. The dream wants you to pay attention to what is causing you these insecurities and to face them and deal with them in a way that puts your waking mind and vulnerability at rest. If you do this you will find that the nightmares will stop.

Premonitions
Dreams that carry warnings or offer glimpses of disasters are known as premonitions. These dreams can leave you feeling helpless with the information presented, as there is a feeling of the events being fated to happen without prevention of any kind. The only way to look at this if you have a premonition and you

know you cannot intervene would be that you have been given some kind of preparation to deal with the events unfolding. This can give you a chance to put things into perspective and to deal with your emotions and maybe help out in some way after the outcome has happened, you can pray or send healing. If you have a premonition of a fatal airplane crash, and have no other information, then you have tuned into the energy vibrations in the build up of such a tragic event. Tragic events about to happen will hold strong energy imprints that make it easier to pick up because of the depth of emotion involved. Maybe you can help the victims families in some way, or you can help others to understand that there is life after death and open their hearts and minds to this truth. If nothing else positive can be gained out of the tragic event, you may realize that your dreams, visions and psychic abilities can prevent this kind of thing from happening to you.

Vivid Dreams

Vivid dreams are those that leave their impression on you in a way that you take notice to what the dream is trying to tell you, for when you are awake. To understand the dream you have to try and decipher the meaning or code work of the symbols in the dream. Here we are not talking about the day's events that unfold in mumbo jumbo style, as the intent there is to clear your conscious mind of the memories and to store what is needed into the sub-conscious. You need to take a look at each object or symbol in the dream one at time and use your vibes to feel and sense what the true meaning is. For instance let's say that you are driving a car and you are having problems steering and cannot seem to control the car or bring it to a stop.

You need to go back into the dream and notice how you feel and what significance the car and the problems steering mean. The car with the faulty steering and breaking system represents you and how you feel you have no control over the future plans unfolding in your life. The steering implies you find it difficult to make a decision regarding your immediate future and the breaks are signifying a need to slow down and evaluate your present circumstances. If you put the clues together, you will find that you need to take stock of your life in the present moment by not rushing ahead into the future through making rash decisions. There is a need to slow down and contemplate your life choices. This can help to regain control of your life and so the dreams will stop. These kinds of dreams can be recurring dreams if the information given is ignored, to stop them from recurring try and decipher the dream and its symbols by going back over the dream and noticing how your vibes feel with each object or situation. Every aspect of the dream is supposed to represent you in some way and this is why you need to use your vibes to decipher the clues. There are many dream books available that explain the meanings of symbols in dreams, but you need to remember, this is a point of reference as each symbol can have a different meaning to individual people. Use your vibes to discover what the symbols mean to you, before you look in any book.

Visitations

The last kind of dreams are visitation dreams and these are when spirit people, your loved ones who have passed on, come back to reveal themselves to you. These are very popular dreams and most people have dreamt of a loved one who has died that they miss dearly. In these dreams the loved one can appear without making any kind of conversation with the intent of saying, "look I am alright". Your dream may be filled with unusual information that is irrelevant but includes your loved one, again the message here is that your deceased loved one has survived physical death and is fine and well in the world of the spirit. Sometimes they will give you a message of hope or to let you know something specific but the main reason is to show you, they have survived death of the physical body.

I have dreamt of my maternal grandmother. She was in her old house on earth coming down her stairs. I was so happy in my dream – another sign with strong emotions being an indication of a visitation – and said to my grandmother, "Nan, what are you doing here? I know you have died!" She replied that, yes she might have died but she can still come and visit with me and was coming to see I was all right. On leaving, my grandmother went to go back up the stairs and I tried to follow her, she told me that I could not go with her as I needed to stay where I was. It was my understanding in the dream and on waking that this meant I could not go with her to her home in the spirit world as my life was still on earth. Those of you who have quite vivid dreams and remember them, will be strong in the ability of clairvoyant vision.

Imagination and Visualization

So we have established that we receive information in the forms of symbols or clues from the subconscious mind in our dream state. Now we are going to look at how we receive psychic information in our waking state, like the dreams it can be through actual or symbolic information. First of all we need to do a little psychic exercise to prepare us for receiving our psychic vibes. This helps to ground us for the work and protect us from unwanted energies. Imagination, intent and visualization are the tools that you will be using for this exercise.

Visualization is simply controlling the imagination to work for you through your intentions, unlike when you meditate and let any information float through your mind. When I ask you to visualize, you construct an image from your subconscious memories of what you have stored away that represents what I have asked you to create. An example of this is if I asked you to visualize a golden pen, your mind will scan for any information that brings up the correct image needed to create the picture for you to recognize. Do not think that you cannot visualize as you definitely can, it may be that it is more subtle than you were expecting and so you are unaware that you are already doing it. The more you experiment with visualization exercises, the stronger and more efficient you will become. Just before you fall asleep at night, images tend to become more prominent because you are in a deep state of relaxation. Notice them, let them pass by and realize that you have the ability to see images within your mind.

Your Spiritual Helpers

Now you are starting the psychic practices, you need to be aware of your spiritual team of helpers they will assist you and protect you through your psychic development. You have a guardian angel who was assigned to you before you were born, with the intent of watching over you and keeping you safe from harm to prevent you from passing before your time. You also have a guide called a spiritual teacher, who helps provide you with the knowledge and information you need, to guide you along your life's path fulfilling your destiny. These spiritual helpers will assist you whenever you ask them and will provide protection and knowledge to unfold your psychic senses. You will learn more about your spiritual team of helpers, in a later chapter, for now just know that they are there. Now, we are ready to start and it is important to be as relaxed as you can as this will harness your soul power to be able to feel the vibes, let's tune in.

Exercise to Tune In

You can do this pretty quickly as long as you are comfortable and not going to be disturbed. Eventually you will be able to open up and tune in, whether or not there are any noises around you, because you will be able to block them out and detach from them. Get comfortable in a seated position, unplug the phone and let others know you are busy so they do not disturb you. Relax and take a few deep breaths, smile and imagine your whole body releasing any tension that may have stored within. This is a quick and easy exercise for psychic preparation.

I want you now, to imagine and visualize a beautiful white light coming down towards you from high up in the sky and from the universe. The white light can be imagined or done with intent, just knowing that it is working for you if you are having problems visualizing it. This white light is gently falling like soft raindrops onto the top of your head and spilling over the sides of you into your auric bodies and to your feet. Next see the light enter inside of your physical body, filling you up from the top of your head to your toes. Take your attention to your feet and see the light go through the soles of your feet through the floor and into the ground and imagine it travelling to the centre of the earth. You can see it attached to a beautiful crystal and is grounding you to the earth plane. Tell yourself that you are now grounded between heaven and earth. Now we say a quick prayer something like this but you can choose one that suits you best. "Dear guides and angels, please protect me as I use my psychic vibes and help me to understand what I receive. I ask this in the name of God, Amen".

What you have done is protected and grounded yourself ready for psychic work which is extremely important, as well as stating your intention to use your vibes, also asking for guidance to decipher the meanings. If you do this every time you use your vibes, your sub-conscious mind automatically knows you are about to do psychic work and you form a commitment and habit. It is always wise to protect yourself and we will deal with this issue in a later chapter on ghosts and hauntings. Do not fear anything remain as relaxed as possible because it is in this state of relaxation that you will be able to receive the information clearly. This is a psychic exercise but in a later chapter we will explore some information on the chakras and how to open up to the spirit world to use mediumship.

For this particular exercise, know that you are only reading psychically and have no intention of communicating with a spirit. You will not be able to run before you can walk and should expect to ground yourself with many psychic exercises to gain valuable experience and understanding, before you decide to develop mediumship.

Clairvoyance

We have now prepared to use our vibes by tuning in, so we need to know what to expect. This is going to be an easy exercise and I will help you along the way by giving you some gentle questions encouraging your vibes to offer you the information. Remember that your sixth sense is a subtle natural sense and is not of the material world and so you are connecting to a believing before seeing sense. You do not see with your physical eyes, you see with your inner vision or what is called the third eye. This energy centre sits between the eyebrows and is activated with psychic work and the images that you see in this centre are delivered by clairvoyance or what is called clear seeing with the inner eye. Symbols and actual information are shown in this centre and there is a need to interpret the pictures to give us clues as to what the message is. This is just one of the ways that you will pick up psychic vibes when you read an item of jewellery.

Clairsentience

Another way of using your vibes will be in feeling strong emotions that are picked up from the item you intend to read. This can affect you for a couple of seconds or so and can happen in a number of ways. Your vibes can pick up emotions in the form of empathy for the person because they may be suffering in some way with depressive or low thoughts. You may also pick up feelings to do with the person's health, as one of my students did when she felt her index finger was very sore when she held another students ring. The one who owned the ring did indeed have a sore index finger that had been hurting her all day, so the student who tuned into the energy vibrations actually felt the pain. This pain disappears as soon as the student mentions it as it does not truly belong to them and is only felt through the psychic ability of clairsentience. All strong emotional reactions can be picked up through using this psychic sense, like with anger, sadness and guilt along with more positive feelings like joy, happiness and excitement too. Clairsentience is known as clear sensing, experiencing inner feelings using your vibes.

Clairaudience

The next sense that you will also experience when using your psychic vibes will be the sense of inner hearing or what is known as clairaudience. Thoughts will pop into your mind that are not yours and they can come as specific words, names or dates and will be experienced in the same way as when I ask you to say your own name in your mind right now. The difference being you are tuned into the object and your attention and intention is on reading this and so you create a psychic link to be able to receive the thoughts from it. This is why the senses are so natural, if you are waiting for some sort of concrete evidence of the psychic senses you will be waiting a very long time. They are so subtle that you can miss them if you are not relaxed enough or by expecting too much. At the moment these are the senses that we will be working with, clairvoyance, clairaudience and clairsentience but be aware for any tastes, smells, or any intuitive flashes of wisdom that you may also pick up on.

When you are ready take an object of jewellery or something that belongs to the person that you have decided to read for. Obviously you have already asked for their permission, it is wise to ask someone that you do not know too much about as your rational mind can get in the way. This can confuse the situation because you try to analyse the information if you assume it may be wrong.

Next get a pen and paper, to record the vibes you pick up so you can check the information later to see how well you have done. I always advise my students to keep a journal anyway to record any vibes they may receive so they can keep a check on their progress. Remember you will be using the main psychic senses of clear seeing, clear hearing and clear sensing. Hold the object in your hand and place your full awareness onto and into it with intent.

I am going to ask you five questions and then you are going to see what you can get on your own.

What are you feeling from this object? In other words what are you feeling from the person who owns the object because their vibes are all over it. You are tuning into the person via the object and have now got your connection with intent. Now, go one step further and ask for more feelings on the person's character or personality. You can gain a lot of information about the person in this way and get to see the real person and not the mask they may be wearing. Are you picking up any kind of health complaint or aches and pains? When you tune into how a person feels, you connect with their mind, body and soul. You are using the psychic sense of clairsentience when you do this.

Ask in your mind to be given a male name that is important to the person who owns the object. This is getting you to receive information by clairaudience – you will receive names, by them popping into your head. You can feel like you are imagining some names, if they are already important to you, but trust your vibes and say them anyway as they may be very accurate indeed.

Ask to be given an important female name and again give what you get even if you think the name belongs to you.

Next, tune into what kind of likes this person has, an example of this can be their hobbies, maybe they love reading or walking in the countryside or sitting at their favourite coffee shop. You could use the psychic sense of clairvoyance here as images may be shown in your mind to give you clues. They can be actual images or symbolic, use your vibes to find out.

Last question see if you can pick up anything that may be connected to the work they do or if you can actually tell what it is they do for a living. It does not matter how you receive the information as long as you are noticing it and jotting it down on paper to check later. Now before you finish see if you get any other information coming to you from the vibes and try to notice, which way you received it. Did you have any intuitive flashes or any fancy smells? You may even pick up on tasting something that is significant to the vibes of the person.

So now you have given five answers, you need to check to see how much you picked up psychically. Practice makes perfect and through practice you will learn to decipher the vibes that you are picking up compared to your own imagination. You even build your own psychic alphabet held in your sub-conscious, to give you instant information when reading for others. Usually, the first things that pop into your mind are your psychic vibes but you can still let your imagination get in the way. What you need to do if this happens is to clear your mind and tune in again by simply focusing with intent in reading the object and then you will link back into the person's energy for you to feel the vibes.

Now that you have finished the exercise you are going to use another kind of visualization exercise to end your practice session. You do this so you can cleanse away any absorbed energy that does not belong to you and this will help to keep you strong, stable and grounded when you have finished. The tuning out exercise will help to control your psychic vibes to establish some form of routine in a safe and gentle manner. By staying in control of the psychic senses you stop yourself from becoming drained and affected by other people's energy or the floating residual energy around you. If you are constantly open you will become tired, low and irritable and your vibes will also attract at this state. The exercise used to end the session, prepares the mind and so a habit is created and expectation is set to switch off and become grounded back into the material world. If you are light headed, easily stressed and over emotional, doing the exercise below will help to bring you back into balance.

Exercise to Tune Out

Imagine by visualization or with intent that you are now being cleaned out with the beautiful white light of the universe. See it washing over you like when you take a shower, make it a powerful shower cleaning you inside and out from your head to your toes into every cell of your body as well as entering every part of your aura. Ask that any stresses or strains now leave you and any other energies that you may have absorbed, be released through the souls of your feet down your grounding cord that you previously attached to the crystal, into the centre of the earth to be changed into neutral energy. Once you have done this drop the light from your feet and let it fall to the centre of the earth so it is detached from you and stays there. Do this with intent or visualization (imagination). Now visualize the white light form a bubble around you, under your feet and over your head with the intention of covering your aura, then fill your bubble up with your favourite colour. Thank your spirit team of helpers for protecting you and helping you with your vibes. To add to your grounding and coming back to reality, you can also make yourself a drink and something to eat. This helps the body function back to earthly matters in the here and now.

White Light

If you can get into a habit of doing this then you will always be protected from unwanted energies and you will be able to do so quickly within minutes as it will become second nature. Thank your guides and angels for their assistance even if you were unaware of them, you can be sure they will be helping out from their side. I also thank God for my own personal reasons and you are welcome to do this in your own way. Congratulate yourself because you have just completed your first psychic exercise in a safe and controlled manner. Keep practicing in this way on objects and you will be preparing your vibes to move onto reading places and people. The most important piece of advice a psychic needs to remember is the use of the white light. White light will keep your energy safe and will connect you to your spiritual helpers also providing you with universal knowledge and wisdom. Each day, get into the habit of surrounding yourself with white light before you go on your travels, you will notice a difference in your health, the way people react to you and your state of mind. White is the colour of purity and contains every colour in the spectrum, therefore cleansing you from any negative energy. Dark energy or what I call negative energy will be repulsed by the white light and will leave you well alone because you are increasing the amount of light within you when you draw this light to you. White light is the light of the Divine and the more light you add to the world the more peaceful and harmonious our planet will become. Every time you raise your vibes you are increasing in the amount of light your aura can hold. You then become a light to others, shining as an example and helping to show them the way.

Sensitivity

The more you understand and use your vibes, the more sensitive you will become. You will notice and receive more information from the universal energy and become more aware of your dreams during sleep. The more spiritual knowledge and wisdom you understand and apply in your life the stronger your vibration becomes. You will increase the divine energy within and your aura will shine brightly, acting as a beacon of light for others to be inspired. You will notice that your relationships with others change as you increase your awareness of the psychic senses. Irritating people, aggressive people, loud and noisy people will leave your life because their vibes do not match yours. Also boring people, depressive people and those who lack ambition and drive will also be unable to match your vibration causing a lack of harmony between you.

The big one is when you are with someone who cannot express how they feel and refuse to communicate their inner truths with you they come across as showing lack of emotional support and openness. All of this will nip away at you because now you are becoming more psychic you are becoming more open and sensitive to others needs, you cannot understand why others are not like you and so you begin to feel different. What is really happening is called spiritual growth all those things that you may not have noticed about people previously are now being brought to your attention because you have done soul work on your self.

You will become sensitive to noise and anything that causes you to feel inner sadness, like with violence or negative news showing on the television or written in the newspapers. I cannot read or watch anything evil or negative as it repulses me and I find it plays on my mind so I would rather not read or watch it in the first place. If you find you are able to detach without having any thing affect you, than that is fine but I assure you the stronger a psychic you get, the less you will be drawn to reading or watching anything negative. You choose what to pay attention to and I choose to pay attention to the best possible vibes I can, therefore creating my life with light and not darkness. This does not mean I ignore any important issues in the world, as I can offer prayer and other forms of help or assistance from a point of light and love and not from fear or darkness.

We are all part of a large collective energy field that merges with each other through energy exchanges and then felt through our individual vibes. The environment, in which we live, will contain the collective energy of all who interact there and this can have an impact on us if we let it. We are spirit people in a physical body and so we are connected to each other in this way. We have different experiences but all belong to the same source. Some people are further along the spiritual path than others through self-awareness and knowledge and this brings more patience and understanding for all people who are spiritually sleeping. You will feel less judgemental about others lives and how they refuse to take responsibility for the pain their in, because you know they are on a journey travelling in their own time at their own pace. They have the same gifts as you do but they refuse to acknowledge and use them until they are ready to accept them, relying only on their five senses.

Relationships and Harmony

You may also find that relationships you have outgrown may break up if your partner does not have the same outlook and understanding of life and refuses to grow with you. Five sensory people tend to mix together and so six sensory people either find partners with the same kind of vibration, or many decide to be independent and live alone until they find the one who shares their spiritual awareness. You have heard of the term, he or she is not on my wavelength, this means they do not share the same physical, emotional or spiritual qualities. If you are in a family that does not share your understanding, they may cause conflict with your new way of being, this will determine how much time, energy or patience you have for them or the development of your psychic senses. I am grateful that my family has always believed in what I do, as this has made things a lot easier for me, but I have seen the other side of things, when lack of belief and encouragement can be shown. This can cause the developing psychic a lot of sadness and a feeling of not belonging to the family unit and can halt or disrupt the development of the psychic senses.

You hear it said that 'opposites attract' and yes, that can be the case but they hardly ever last and if they do, it would not be a deep soul mate relationship because one would not be in harmony with the other. 'Like attracts like' has more of a chance of an everlasting relationship. Of course only you know if you desire to stay in a relationship or not and cannot control the intentions of your partner. This is why falling in love can be a big risk, for you must open your heart and soul, to let love in knowing that one day maybe your loved one could change their feelings for you. We have all heard the quote 'it is better to have loved and lost than to never have loved at all'. True love is love that touches the soul not just the heart, hearts can be broken but the souls love is eternal. To be a successful psychic it is important to have an open heart as having compassion, unconditional love and understanding is all part of a psychics work. I would also like to point out, that many people seek the guidance off a psychic because of relationship problems so the more you understand about harmony, balance and matching vibes, the more accurate your predictions will be.

Soul Mates

There is someone out there for everyone and we attract them to us through our vibes so the more we learn to love ourselves and accept ourselves then we open our vibes up to receive the love that we deserve. People who are afraid of being hurt in love will block their heart and therefore block attracting the right kind of love into their life. They fear getting hurt before they even let a new relationship begin and therefore feel they must somehow be, unlucky in love. Luck has nothing to do with it, as it is the state of your vibes through your true inner feelings that allow love to enter or to stay away. Soul mates are spirits that have known each other from before this earth-plane existence. Soul mates do not have to be involved in a marriage or a sexual relationship for they can exist, between family members or friends that hold a special kind of rapport and bond. These are your spirit friends that you remember and recognize through your vibes at an un-conscious level. They are part of your individual journey on earth for what ever reason being, as well keeping you company along your path. You will be reunited again when you pass over to the spirit world along with all the other people who you love that has been apart of your life here on earth.

Knowing this helps you to feel less fearful about dying and helps you to live the best life you can live, whilst on earth because you know your vibes will be available for all to read when you pass over. My soul mates on earth have been my grandfather Jack who passed away when I was little but we had a great bond that is still with me now from beyond the grave. Also my husband Jock, who has the same understanding of spiritual and psychic knowledge as I do, I feel it was absolute destiny to meet him and feel we arranged it before we were born. I also have soul friends and a special bond with my nephew Liam, who I love as if he were my own child. Look around you, who do you have a special bond with? You will feel like you have known them from before and will have a deep inner love for them that touches your soul. All this knowledge about people, relationships and life will help you to discover a theme with potential clients needing guidance by giving you a deeper understanding of how they feel inside.

Use your Vibes

You can help your vibes become a natural part of your daily life for once activated you will see the potential that comes with using them. Never again will you just rely on the five senses, you will use your psychic senses along side of your fives senses to enhance your life and future. This book is more than psychic development, this book also helps you to remember who you are and the divine power that is within you. You are spirit in human form; you came from spirit and when it is your time to pass you will go back to spirit. You have a life purpose and a destiny and this book will help you to find out what that may be. For one you would not have picked up this book if you were not ready to receive the information within its pages. Your vibrations attracted the book to you through the energy that you gave out. Part of everyone's life purpose is to remember who they really are, and you have achieved this through receiving this book. Now you have read this chapter, you will have gained an inner awareness of vibes, how they work and life with the psychic senses. A psychic is someone who feels information and taps into the subtle vibrations of energy that exists beyond the physical senses. Read the notes below to help you remember the important points of this chapter.

Vibes Check List

- Our vibes are affected by our thoughts and feelings – happiness and listening to your heart, will create good vibes stress and focussing on problems will create bad vibes. Remember you will attract more of the same towards you.

- Know that you are a soul who is eternal and containing a Divine Spark of God. This means you have creative power to be tapped into with the psychic senses to use to make wiser life choices and create the unfolding of desires.

- Become aware of your dreams and notice to see if they are providing you with any information. Write down your dreams and go through the symbols one at a time, then use your vibes to feel what they mean.

- Protect yourself with the exercises provided before you do any psychic work and then remember to close down and cleanse. Always use white light daily, it will build up your spiritual connection and strengthen your vibes. Ask your spirit team of
- helpers to protect and assist you when using your vibes.

  Practice your psychometry by reading objects and try reading new things like photographs or touching old buildings to see what you pick up. Remember that psychometry is used to tap
- into and link with the past and present experiences.

  Remember when using your psychic senses to record any images or symbols, thoughts and feelings as well as any names
- that pop into your mind. Build up your psychic alphabet.

  Notice the people in your life and see if there are any changes, through people leaving your life and new friends coming in. Look to see if you have any soul mate relationships in your life for they have always been with you from life before in the
- spirit world or from past lives.

- Keep a journal to record your vibes and notice improvements made through practice and time, this will help you to gain confidence in your psychic development and help bring accuracy and success.

CHAPTER TWO

Intuition

To be a successful psychic, you need to be able to trust your vibes. I will show you quick and easy ways for you to start gaining the trust in yourself, so you can tune into energy vibrations, feel them, then read them. You will also see the benefits of why healing your vibes can help to produce faith and trust in yourself, giving you an awareness to understand and help others. The major way in which we feel the vibes is through our intuition. Intuitive flashes of wisdom or inspiration coming to you instantaneously as a knowing, is what can be understood as intuition. Intuition is a knowing and feeling sense, our feelings can be produced internally with our emotions or with physical sensations of the body.

Understanding and acknowledging our feelings is a very important aspect of developing and strengthening our intuition. We can help to do this through living in the present moment, being aware of our surroundings, choices and actions, so that we can give our energy our full attention and focus.

Intuition is also known as our gut instinct and as the name suggests can produce funny feelings in the stomach area. An example of this is when you are excited and have nervous energy and you feel the sensation of what is termed 'butterflies' in the tummy. This is the area where you can feel anxiety and fear or an inner sensation of uneasiness, sometimes even nausea. You also feel the excitement of falling in love in this area, especially when you talk to or meet up with your loved one your tummy flutters. There are a number of different careers that rely on using intuition in their jobs, for instance the police will say they have a hunch about something or have an uneasy feeling in the pit of their stomach. A mother will have a strong intuitive bond with her children and often know when something is wrong. Medical staff who are stuck on a diagnosis have been known to say, "I don't know what it is, but something is telling me it could be this that's wrong". Therefore intuition can be expressed with physical sensations in your body to get your attention about something or it can come as insight through inspiration and intuitive flashes of wisdom.

Physical Intuitive Feelings

Intuitive feelings that are expressed physically are produced because an energy exchange of information has taken place that the soul has absorbed and interpreted to the physical body through intuition to get its attention. The body then expresses its symptoms, helping the conscious mind to take notice and be alert. The stomach isn't the only area where we feel the vibes, our hair can stand on end, our muscles can twitch, we can shiver or have palpitations along with a change in breathing patterns and we can also experience an overall feeling of uneasiness. All of these signs expressed in the body are to alert us of imminent danger or in making unwise decisions. If we pay attention to the way our body is feeling we may prevent ourselves from experiencing harm as well as having repercussions from unwise choices. The more we listen too and act on the subtle nudges of the intuition, the stronger our intuitive vibes become. This helps our intuition to produce the best results or solutions for our highest good. How many times have you decided to do something even though, you had an uneasy feeling or knowing sensation that things would go array and then found after, that is exactly what happened? You would have told yourself, "I knew that was going to happen" you then wish you had listened.

Intuitive Feelings

Sometimes you will find that you seem to just know things before they happen without understanding how you could have obtained this information. I was eight years old when I first became aware of my intuition although I didn't realize what it was. I had been having a drink of orange squash and didn't finish it all, so I placed my plastic cup half full in the fridge. A few hours later I decided to go back and finish it up and on opening the fridge door I knew instantly that a spider was floating in my drink. How did I know? I hadn't even opened the door. I felt an overall sense of knowing not to drink it without looking in it because there was a spider in there. Then I looked in and I saw a spider floating in my squash. I swear I didn't know what I was more shocked about, the fact that a spider was in my drink, as I am not too keen on spiders, or the fact that I knew about it before I even looked. I screamed and dropped the squash and that was the first time I became consciously aware of the sixth sense.

There have been many times throughout my life when I have had an overall sense of knowing not to do something and have listened to my feelings and because of this, have saved myself from upset and hurt. Intuition speaks strongly if it is a spur of the moment decision or a compulsion to do something that may not be a wise choice and so instant intuition kicks in with pre-warnings to alert you. These feelings can come in different ways, they can be strong ones like when you have received a shock, an adrenaline rush flows throughout your body. You can become filled with an overall sense of dread and unease or you can receive the feelings from a gentle knowing deep inside of you that if you follow through on your choice you will be making a big mistake. The gentle knowing you receive is linked to your higher self, who quickly impresses you with the best information and understanding instantaneously. You can also experience wonderful inner feelings, calmness or excitement that helps to confirm with you that you are doing the right thing.

A True Intuitive Story

Les is a student of mine and Jock's and has developed as a wonderful healer, he enjoys meditating a lot and through this and his state of mind has developed his intuitive side quite naturally. Les was enjoying a leisurely walk alone not so long ago and was quite surprised to be suddenly overcome with feelings of dread along with strong physical sensations throughout his body. He knew to pay attention to these feelings but was unaware on looking around him what the actual problem was. Next minute a jeep came hurtling around the corner at such an incredible speed that its two wheels nearly came off the road and Les had to quickly step aside and missed being hit by inches. I asked Les if he felt the feelings he received had helped him to survive being hurt. Les replied that if he had not received those feelings he would have been paying attention to the scenery around him and so just a couple of seconds caught off guard could have caused him his life or the very least from being badly hurt. Paying attention to your intuition can save your life. Every time you listen to your intuition you are building an inner rapport with your sixth sense and strengthening your instincts to work for you for your highest good.

Universal Signs

The universe will also use any means possible to grab your attention and at the right moment in time you may find yourself meeting the right person needed to help you along your life path because you have picked up on the signs. Synchronistic events may happen, leading up to you meeting the love of your life in making sure that your paths cross. The words that you need to hear can be spoken out of a strangers mouth making something inside of you just click into place helping you know what you need to do next in your life. The message in a film you have just enjoyed may inspire you to take action in your life to make the changes that are needed. There are many ways in which the universe can speak to you via your intuition you just need to be aware of the signs and synchronicities unfolding through listening to the language of your soul. Synchronicities and miracles can happen and unfold when intuitive flashes of inspiration are followed. Great works of art have been created when inspiration has been ignited through the soul along with wonderful words of wisdom written in books and poems to help inspire the multitude who read them. Two people at opposite sides of the world can be inspired with the same creative idea at the same time because their intuition tapped into the signs of the universe.

Your angel and guide can communicate to you through your intuitive vibes, as well as your higher self or what is called the voice of your soul. They can do this by producing feelings within you for you to take notice and take action on. They can also give you information by placing thoughts within your head, gently influencing you so that you think it is your own ideas, and you then have the free will to listen or not. You may hear these thoughts form a sentence or you could have information in your mind or you could be filled with an instantaneous knowing from out of nowhere. I call this an 'aha moment', an epiphany or a light bulb going off inside your head. All of a sudden you are aware of what you need to do or say because of an intuitive flash of inspiration and you find that it is exactly what is needed for the best outcome.

Loved ones in spirit can also give you gentle influences for your highest good so you can make wiser life choices or prevent you from facing danger. Life presents us with plenty of opportunities and chances to progress and receive what we want, bringing happiness and fulfilment into our lives. We can easily miss out on these opportunities by not paying attention to the signs and nudges of our intuition. The universe will always provide you with everything you truly want in the desires of the heart and soul. They do this by supplying you with the tools and information needed for you to create your vision or goal in your own unique way using the responsibility of your free will and creative spark. If you take no action and then wait for things to happen, you will miss out on the gifts of the universe.

An example of this, if you desire more money, the universe is not going to drop five thousand dollars into your lap, or provide you with the lottery numbers, no! They will bring you ways in which you can help yourself to create the sum of money desired. If you ignore or miss the opportunities, signs or the right people brought your way to assist you, then you miss out on understanding and trusting what listening to the intuitive vibes can do for you. Ways that can prevent you from listening to your intuition and receiving exactly what you desire are low vibes from low feelings that keep you from harmonising with your specific wants. In this case you need to take responsibility to heal those low vibes so you can tune into the energy of the universe through your intuition. You will discover more about creating your dreams and goals in a later chapter on using your vibes for manifesting success.

Heal your Vibes

Learn how to heal yourself first, your own perception will colour the way you feel the vibes. The stage of your life development at this moment in time along with all past experiences and knowledge, as well as overcoming any mistakes, will be the catalyst for how you perceive life and trust your vibes. Are you an optimist or a pessimist? Do you see the glass as half full or half empty? This will affect the way in which you interpret any vibes you feel, or act on any intuition you receive. It will also affect the way you will give guidance if you wish to become a professional psychic. No one is perfect and once one aspect of us has been refined, there will always be another that will need polishing up. Healing your vibes should be a constant striving throughout your life, to better yourself and to bring you an overall feeling of total wellbeing balanced in mind, body and spirit.

The more balanced and emotionally refined you are, the more you are able to help others along their path. Each time we overcome something within us, we are then able to use our knowledge and wisdom to help others suffering in the same way. We have been there and done that and healed through it, so we have a good vibe of what the person needs to do, to heal. If you lack confidence, suffer from low-self esteem and have no love or belief in yourself, this will affect the way you trust your vibes. In other words, you will not listen to your intuition and miss out on vital opportunities or chances that can bring deep satisfaction in your life. This is because you do not value your own self or have the belief within you to create great things. Just like an onion can peel away different layers all the way to its core, so do we refine our soul each time we heal a deep hurt, emotional problem or any blockages that hold us back. Healing yourself, is having the courage to look within to know the real you. Psychic development is soul development you are refining the gifts of the soul through healing and commitment. A professional psychic will need to be at a certain level of progression and would have healed a lot of hurt within their life so they have the knowledge and guidance to assist others. Your vibes will influence the way you interpret the information received by the way you perceive the world around you because of the sum total of your life's experiences.

One person can go to two different psychics and get two very different readings but both will be accurate. The reason for this is because of the way the psychics own aura and vibes resonate. If they are generally positive they will focus on the best course of action in a reading. If they are negative or pessimistic, they will focus on problems, adversities and stress within the reading. Like I said, both can be accurate in their own way but the one who has a lighter and positive vibration will be more of a helpful and healing psychic, working for the highest good of the client. They are likely to be more accurate and also offer information on a soul level. This is because their vibes are raised enough to channel spiritual guidance, along with a deeper understanding of life. Remember you can block any psychic information from flowing by the negative quality of your vibes. This is because of your emotions, state of mind and lack of understanding of the bigger picture of life.

A professional psychic is someone who is able to detach from their clients problems, so they can offer the best spiritual and psychic guidance possible. If you desire to use your vibes to the best of your abilities, it is wise to fully understand this concept, how can you heal others if you cannot heal yourself. When giving a psychic reading from a detached point of view, you are offering your client an accurate and unbiased reading. It is easy to let the ego slip and our human nature think that it knows best by offering guidance that may not be constructive or helpful in the long run. Five years ago a client came to me for a reading who was being constantly physically abused by her husband. It had been going on for years and she had never left him. My ego felt really sorry for her and wanted to tell her to leave the man – not what I called him in my head – and put an end to this misery. However I knew better and she as we all are, are going through life lessons and must choose our own way. I passed on spiritual information about her soul's journey and explained how change must come from within for it to be experienced without. I like to think that she finally took the courage and left him but I never heard from her again. My vibes tell me she was desperate to leave she just needed to find the confidence within.

Intuitive Guidance
A psychiatrist will detach from their patient so that they can observe the inner emotional pain of their subject and therefore offer the correct treatment instead of merely sympathising with their patient. In psychic work, the same detachment is needed for

the highest good of the client. This means that you may have to tell them things that they are not really wanting to hear. The biggest truth a psychic needs to impress their client with is to take responsibility for creating their life. If a client is only interested in sympathy or just wanting someone to listen to them complaining, then it would be less expensive to talk with their family or friends. People who enjoy going from one psychic to another is refusing to grow or may be unable to take responsibility for their life. Personally I find that the hour I spend with a client is one that will offer them exactly what they need for their highest good to move forward in their life need. I make a point of not giving the same person a reading for at least six months to one year unless truly needed. I try and teach them to trust their own vibes and for them to know they have the power to do this by listening to their intuition.

A true psychic is someone who will offer guidance along ones path making it clear that it is the free will of the client to use this guidance or not. As a psychic, I make it clear to my clients who are in the state of self pity and feeling hard done by, that they need to take action to make the changes they want. Sometimes this advice can fall on deaf ears and the client can expect me to give them wonderful news without any action on their part. I call this the 'magic wand theory' as they think I have the power to make their lives happy through what I predict. I do not give my clients what it is they want to hear, I give my clients what it is they need to hear and for their highest good. I can channel information from their guides, angels and loved ones in spirit, who have been trying to help them wake up and smell the coffee. Most of the time I know that the spirit world are trying to reach them through me but at the end of the day the client's own free will can ignore this advice or take it on board.

To be unbiased and detached from the problems, will help your vibes become clearer offering accurate information. If your emotions get in the way of your vibes, then you can be off in your interpretations and predictions or become muddled and confused in understanding any information received. Mastering the emotions will help you to master trusting your vibes.

Other People's Vibes

Have you ever sat by yourself in a coffee shop, sipping your coffee and watching the world go by? The reason I ask, is that it is something that many a psychic loves to do, including myself. When you are aware of other people, as a silent witness, you can learn so much about the way peoples energy fields affect them. This is not being nosy as you are not infringing in their private lives, you are merely noticing how different energy fields exist. If you try this, you will notice how you are automatically sensing their auras by just placing your focus, awareness and intention on them. Some people will seem to glow and shine and be happy in their body, not just by smiling or laughing but in the whole way that they carry themselves, their eyes sparkle and their exude a friendly open aura. Others will look like they carry the weight of the world on their shoulders, they are filled with stresses and strains and their aura reflects this. They will not have as welcoming an aura as the happy one and can feel stand offish and closed. What you are doing when you bring your attention to the present moment, is training your mind to focus and become self-aware enhancing your intuition to work for you. It is important to live in the present and not worry about the past or the future. If you are using some of your energy to worry about the past or future, you will not have all of your awareness in the here and now to help you feel your vibes completely. The more you notice others energy, the more you learn to trust your vibes and intuitive feelings as you gain an inner knowing of the psychic senses.

Exercise to Enhance Your Intuition

For this exercise you are going to need to make notes within your journal building up your psychic alphabet of feelings, meanings and interpretations for you to understand your own development and how you work with your intuition. You need to pick at least five people you know, each with different personalities so you can begin to discover how different people evoke different emotions within you. This is going to help you when you meet new people for the first time, as feelings are produced through your intuitive vibes that offer you the story of what they are truly like. These feelings are stored inside you from every person or situation you have ever come across in your life so far, you are going to learn to bring them to the surface to use them. You will be tuning into the real person behind any mask they may wear. To gain a deeper trust of your intuition listen to the heart as this is the seat of the soul. Ask yourself, what is your heart feeling? Then have the courage to act on these feelings and soon your intuition will flourish. That is the secret to feeling the vibes.

Just white light yourself quickly with intent and you are ready.

Now you are ready to pick one person at a time to give your complete attention and focus too. This is going to help you to link into their energy and produce a feeling within you about how 'they make you feel'. An example, if I choose to give my attention to someone who is very loving and caring, I am focusing on them and the feelings and emotions that are evoked within me from this person. I may feel a warm and glowing sensation, a happy feeling or a safe and secure feeling. What I would record in my psychic journal, would be all of these feelings so that if I meet someone new and they make me feel the same way, I know I would be able to trust them or at least feel at ease in their company. We all vibe people out unconsciously and have met people that we just seem to click with and feel like we have known them all of our lives and yet we also meet others we do not like even though we have not yet got to know them. We are not judging them though as what we are doing is receiving information via their aura to ours and our intuition is interpreting the signals they are emitting and so we form our conclusion. The problems happen when we ignore our intuitive vibes and find that we are let down and cheated and feel disappointed that we should have known better. This exercise will help you to be conscious of what your intuition receives.

- First pick someone who has love for you and write down how this person makes you feel, remember the feelings evoked can be physical or emotional.

- Now pick someone who is fun and write down all feelings that come from how this person makes you feel, keep repeating the exercise for the rest below.

- Next pick a person who is angry.

- Next pick a person who gives you the creeps.

- Next pick a person who is not on your wavelength – they could be five sensory or even sceptical.

Now you have written these vibes within your journal keep building them up if you come across any new feelings that you receive from, other people. Make sure you connect to how 'they make you feel', when they occupy your energy. Your aura and their aura will come into contact with each other and information is automatically absorbed and interpreted to the intuition. If you become aware of how people make you feel, you will have instantaneous results from the intuition to help you decide to spend time with them, understand them or even prevent you from spending time with someone who is less than reputable in their actions.

The exercise can also help when you need information on:

- Interviewing someone for a job or work within the home – example, live-in nanny, domestic cleaner, a partner for your business or employee, wedding planner or anyone who is hired for your own personal reasons. You can vibe them out to see if they are as qualified as they claim to be or are suitable for your needs.

- Going out on a date – to vibe out whether or not your partner is someone who is reliable, honest and sincere and if they are on your wave length or not.

- Someone tries to sell you insurance or any kind of financial investment – use your vibes to check if they are hiding any important information by noticing how they make you feel. The classic salesman who stands out like a sore thumb to someone who is in tune with their intuition is the car sales man. I love to vibe people out and car sales man are the funniest as they are trained to sell cars by doing what they can and learn all the tricks in the book. They may be able to sustain this act with five sensory people but you can never lie to a psychic because no matter what you pretend to be the real you is always revealed within the aura. On the surface they come across as extremely helpful, kind and trusting but I can feel what is going on inside them and to me they feel like a stoat or weasel like the ones in 'Wind in the Willows' the film. I can see them clasping their hands, licking their lips and thinking 'yum dinner!', as they go in for the kill, counting up their commission. I will admit not all car salesmen are like this but I have come across quite a few. Trust your intuition as it always has your best interests at heart and you can save yourself from buying an old banger for an outrageous price.

Basically, you can use your vibes with anyone who comes into your life to vibe them out for your own benefit which can prevent you from experiencing problems through being too naïve and trusting without knowing the real person. You can save yourself from getting hurt, let down and also getting ripped off financially. There have been many instances where people have been cheated and lied to by their partners, either with a third party involved or with the intent of conning them out of their life savings. Bigamists and con artists will be charming, loving and pretend to be sincere but remember, vibes never lie and you can never lie to a psychic as trusting your intuition can reveal the truth of their real selves. All that false pretence will fall away to reveal the lying, cheating and manipulative intent of who they really are.

I love to vibe people out for the first time and have saved myself, time, stress and worry by listening to my intuition. I have been lied to and have known immediately and have had the courage to say to the person, "you are not telling me the truth". This usually takes them aback and I follow up by saying, "you do know I am psychic". You should see the faces of my friend's partners when my friends tell them, 'Jo can tell when someone is lying and cheating...' all being said with a little giggle.

Intuitive Decisions

You have been given the psychic secret in how to trust your vibes with people, now I am going to show you how to use your vibes to help you make wiser decisions. Everyday we make constant choices that affect our lives. Some decisions we make will bring us the rewards we wanted, where others will end up making us regret we made them. Wouldn't it be handy to have complete faith in knowing that what we choose is going to work out best for us? Well using your vibes to help you make decisions is like having someone older and wiser on hand encouraging you all the way. To make the best decisions, you need to have the confidence and trust in yourself to make the changes within your life.

You have already been given some knowledge on how to heal your vibes to make you feel better about yourself and for you to believe in yourself. By listening to your vibes and having the courage to take action, can help you to increase in confidence and also help you to realize you are capable of being and doing anything you truly desire. Only you hold yourself back or move yourself forward, no one else is responsible for your state of mind and individual vibrations.

To make the best overall decisions it is important to notice if you are listening to the signs of the universe. If you have decided to do something and you notice that instant opportunities have presented themselves through so called coincidences, then pay attention because this is a clear sign that help is there for you from source energy to make your idea become a reality. This is you going with the flow of the universe where you are in tune with life, your vibes act naturally to tap into the help you need to accomplish your goal. You have an overall sense that you are on the right path. However, if you are coming up against one obstacle after another, then you need to revaluate your life circumstances and look towards a new direction or different desire. Sometimes what we think we want is not actually what we really need and so doors will be closed and we will be given the opportunity to think things over. If we take action things will improve for us but if we fight against those closed doors we will delay and prolong our frustration and unhappiness. If your life is flowing with ease then you can be sure you are listening to your intuition. We all experience problems and obstacles in our lives but when you listen to your intuition you are helping yourself face these problems and deal with them far easier than if you bury them causing blocks within your life.

Is your decision going to cause upset and pain to someone intentionally? I am not talking about walking away from a relationship as obviously this is painful for both parties, I am talking about intent to get revenge or hurt someone. If so then you will receive a temporary satisfaction that will soon end up back firing and will bring even more pain back to you when your emotions return back to normal. For every cause there is an effect, this is the spiritual law of 'what goes around comes around' and what you give out to others, gets returned back to you. Live from the goal, 'do unto others as you would have others do unto you' and you will not go far wrong.

Balancing karma is controlled through your own actions, feelings and intent and every decision you make you will be accounted for. Use your intuition to see how it sits in your soul, ask yourself if your morals and conscience are able to cope with unwise decisions you can save yourself from many regrets if you do this. When you are choosing something try and choose it for the highest good of all, this means that you are being responsible for your actions as well as realising how your actions can affect others along the way. If something doesn't sit right with you then you are probably being given the intuitive vibes to alter and change your course of action. Use this next exercise to help you use your intuition to make decisions.

Exercise to Trust Intuition for Instant Decisions

To choose a holiday

Decide where you want to go, and then collect information on this destination.

Now within your mind, imagine you are already there, how does it make you feel? Is there something missing, do you feel uncomfortable and is the place you have chosen to stay at making you feel safe and secure? These are just some of the things you can ask in your mind to produce immediate emotional or physical reactions. If you get good vibes then you know that this is a good choice to follow.

To go on a night out

You have been invited out to dinner with a group of friends, imagine you are already there and again check your emotional reactions. If you feel that the evening will be a disaster for what ever reasons then trust your vibes and cancel, you can always get feed back from those who went to discover how the evening panned out. It could be that you saved yourself from distress because of the travel there or back. Check in with your intuition to feel the vibes you receive as you use visualization to run through the evening.

To change jobs

You are fed up in you current job and want something different, you have a job offer but are unsure if you should take it or not just encase you end up regretting it. Usually your rational mind would talk you out of it to prevent you from taking a risk but you allow your vibes to scan how the new job would make you feel. You tune into what is expected of you and anything that you can associate with the job then you notice how your emotions are reacting to your visualizations. If you feel good vibes then you can be sure if you didn't accept the job, you would be missing out on a great opportunity that has presented itself. Obviously if you get bad vibes then you know in your heart that it doesn't feel right with you and will be an unwise choice to take. Remember you can use your vibes to vibe out any important decision, invitation or idea.

Heart over Head

Here is an important piece of advice in how to know if you are making the correct decisions. When you listen to your vibes, your heart will rule your head. This is not preventing the rational mind from helping out in anyway as you still have free will to listen, your heart is making you aware of the best decision. An example – you are in a comfortable relationship with a really nice person, you love them like a family member and there is no passion or chemistry left within the relationship. You heart says you need passion, chemistry and desires to move on, your head says 'you're crazy, this person loves you and if you leave you may never find anyone who is as nice as they are'. Two things can happen here, you can listen to your heart and leave the relationship which can cause temporary pain but once this has subsided will leave you free to finding exactly what stirs your soul and attract the best person for you.

The other thing is that you refuse to leave the relationship, end up not being completely satisfied and happy and probably daydream or fantasize of what you are missing. You go through the motions and every now and then when you are not occupying yourself or keeping yourself busy, you have the same thoughts and feelings about wanting to leave again. Another year goes by and if you are not too careful you will look elsewhere for attention, passion and chemistry. This can be the beginning of an affair that causes pain, guilt and suffering within your vibes. You end up having an extremely painful break up that spoils all chance of friendship remaining as well as having caused more pain to someone than if you had the courage to leave previously. As a psychic, I come across this scenario a lot when my clients come to see me for guidance about their relationships. They want to know if they should leave their partner and if they will be happy if they do? The one thing I say to them is, if you are unhappy and have feelings or fantasises about leaving your partner, then you would not be having these thoughts if you were with the love of your life.

Too many people stay in unhappy relationships, refusing to acknowledge their inner pain and make the decisions that could make them happy once again. I know quite a few people who are living a lie within their relationships and they fear changing their lives because of finances, or other excuses. These people I know will use their vibes for other areas of their lives but cannot face using them to change what is causing them unhappiness. I watch how this affects their lives and see how they cannot live their truth and follow their heart. How can you help others in life if you cannot help yourself with the same advice? You cannot be fully in tune with your intuition if you ignore your own inner feelings because you fear change.

My motto in life is to live your truth and follow your heart, only then can you ever be true to yourself and be able to help others to do the same. The same clients can return to me five years later with the same problems. What does that tell you? It tells me they are wasting an important part of their lives. If you intend to work as a professional psychic, relationship issues will be the most asked questions you will usually come across. This is because love, getting hurt and being afraid to trust or make changes in a relationship can cause the strongest emotional reactions in life. People fear being lonely but also prevent themselves from opening their heart to love for fear of being hurt before they even try. A successful psychic will always follow the voice of their intuition.

Now we have finished this chapter, we are ready to go deeper into psychic development and explore more about the aura, chakras and colour intuition. In the next chapter you will begin to start giving psychic readings to others. Remember the ground work you had to do to prepare your vibes before you are able to help others. You have learned how to tune in and out, plus white light yourself, you have completed psychometry on jewellery and now you understand how intuition can be used to help you in your daily life along with using it to vibe others.

Vibes Check List

- Use your vibes to notice how other people make you feel, this can protect you from being cheated on and lied too.

- Notice how your intuition speaks to you with physical or emotional feelings along with any universal signs. Remember there are no such things as coincidences.

- Make an effort to work on yourself by healing your vibes so you raise your vibrations and have the total understanding and experience to help others along their path.

- Use your vibes to make wiser life choices by visualizing what it feels like to be actually living that choice and notice what you feel is sitting right with you.

- Make decisions based on your highest good and the good of all, remembering that what you give out will be returned to you.

- When making decisions listen to your heart the seat of your soul in comparison with your head that wants to prevent you from taking risks.

- Know that the more you rely on your intuition, the stronger it becomes and soon you will be so in tune with your soul that your life will flow with more ease.

- Write everything down in your journal so you can keep a check on your development, building up your psychic alphabet.

CHAPTER THREE

Colour Vibrations

Colours of the soul can be described as the aura and chakras, you are going to discover a fascinating way in which to read the aura and chakras and give very accurate psychic readings. This is called colour interpretation and we are going to read the colours found in our energy systems to conduct a one on one psychic reading. Remember I said that all information about us can be found within the aura, well reading the colours can start you off in gaining a valuable amount of accurate information. This helps you to focus on colours as a tool, supplying you with the knowledge to interpret the vibes of another person. As you have a tool to start you off, you will develop an inner trust and confidence that will help bring your soul powers and intuitive nature to the surface. This can lead you to develop your psychic senses to an advanced state, where you will be able to read others without using any tools at all. If you find you have a special rapport with reading colours, you may wish to always use them to help start you off at the beginning of a reading. The goal is to use your intuitive vibes and psychic senses along with the colour interpretations to be able to give extra information to the person being read for. This will happen naturally each time you tune in, you will have an overall sense of who the person really is. Both of your energy fields intermingle and your aura obtains the information needed from the other person.

The Aura
The aura around you can expand in every direction and is said to contain seven subtle bodies of energy, each interpenetrating the other and vibrating at different frequencies. With our intention

we can expand the aura to make our presence known or we can draw in our aura close to our physical body for protection and to be as inconspicuous as possible. The aura changes shape and colour with the different feelings and moods that we experience. When we are happy our aura will reflect this, our energy will emit sparkles of light and emit a glow within the whole auric field and a psychic can see this with their clairvoyant vision.

The happier we are our aura will naturally expand as we become the life and soul of the party. Whenever we lighten up our moods, we increase in vibrancy and our aura shines with light. If our moods are low and negative or we feel sad and blue, our aura will show murky colours and weird shapes. The aura will draw closer into the body and not be as vibrant in strength and colour.

Flashes of red in the aura can be from angry thoughts that also cause sharp lines or spikes within the energy flow. If we are in a calm state of mind, our aura will show soft wavy lines along with a lovely soft green colour.

Colour is an amazing attribute to our physical and emotional wellbeing and things like the clothes we wear or the colours we surround ourselves with at home can influence our health and moods because each colour has its own vibration. We can unconsciously choose clothes that contain the colour vibration we need to lift our spirits. If you are tired and need extra energy, you may find yourself picking out something red, as this contains a vibrancy that will increase your own energy levels. If you are in need of healing then you may choose to wear blue and if you need balance you find that you are drawn to wearing green. Look out for those who wear a lot of pink, this is a psychic and sensitive colour and is connected to the heart chakra pink can represent being in love, falling in love or needing to love yourself.

Seeing the Aura

Anyone can learn to see the fist layer or subtle body of the aura the one closest to the physical body by adjusting their focus and vision to look past the person selected. They will see this as a white or grey outline or as a white haze around the physical body. It is best to practice the first time with a white or neutral back round behind the person until you are more adept. In pictures and paintings of Jesus Christ, it shows a halo of light around his head within his aura, representing an enlightened being, this is called a nimbus. The more spiritual knowledge and under-standing you have in life the more light you shine within your aura. One dear friend once said to me a very long time ago, "Joanne you have a lovely light around you, make sure you never let it dim". At the time I did not grasp what she meant, but now I know that she saw in my aura my spiritual essence, passion and happy nature as a vibrant light and she did not want me to lose it. Clairvoyant ability can be used to see further than the first subtle body to see colour, movement and shapes within it, practice makes perfect.

Obtaining Information from the Aura

We are able to receive any information about the person from within their aura, as it contains everything about them from the state of their health to their dreams and desires. Also included within the aura, are all the past lives that our soul has ever experienced, including all lessons learned and knowledge gained, moulding us into the unique individual we are today. The aura can show if a person has confidence or low self esteem and reflects what they truly think about themselves. If they are happy with their self image and generally like who they are, their aura will glow and be dynamic and strong. If they have any self-hatred or negative critical thoughts about themselves then their aura will be weak and shrink as close to the physical body as it can. This can explain how some people are naturally charismatic and others are like wallflowers who stay in the background and would rather not be noticed. You can also receive information about a person's state of mind and physical health from their auric field. We all experience the ups and downs of life and our state of mind effects the colour emanations within our aura. Our state of mind is directly connected to our rate of vibration and a faster lighter vibration requires positive light hearted thoughts. Physical health problems show up within the aura before they manifest within the physical body. A clairvoyant psychic will be able to see the abnormalities of ill health in the etheric body ready to show up in the physical body, unless preventive measures are taken. It is said that the limbs of a person that are missing in the physical body, still show up complete in the etheric body.

Healers can feel this energy in the place where the limb once was, even though it no longer exists. Illness can show in the body as dark murky colours of a low vibration like black, grey and brown. Someone who does not take good care of their health and is overworked, fatigued and drained of energy will express a dull grey lifeless colour. You have heard of the expression, they have lost their spark, if the aura is constantly in this miserable state then depression is likely to set in.

The Chakras

The physical body is the densest of the subtle auric bodies and each body becomes a faster, lighter vibration and frequency the furthest away it moves. The etheric body includes the chakra system also known as psychic centres. Chakra is a Sanskrit word, meaning 'wheel', and there are also seven chakras that connect to the seven subtle bodies of the aura that we will be working with. Other minor chakras exist within our energy system but the seven main ones are our focus for psychic development. They can be likened to vortexes of energy that interpenetrate with the physical body and each one is associated with an endocrine gland or nerve plexus. The colours of the rainbow are also associated with the chakras with each chakra assigned a particular colour. This is why I am going to show you how to interpret the colours for you to connect to the chakras and aura and gain a deeper awareness.

If you want to further your psychic studies, as I know a budding psychic cannot get enough of reading books and attending courses, it is wise to research the areas of the human energy field and chakras. Harry Oldfield is a pioneering scientist on the fringe of exploration into the auric field, its existence and its use in medical applications including health screening, his work is vital in providing evidence of the aura. Studying this information will also help you if you wish to develop the healing side of the spiritual pathway. Using colour will help you to understand more about the chakras and the auric field. I will show you enough in this book for you to become a successful psychic, and the rest is up to you. Below you will find a description of the chakra system including the physical association of each one. Each chakra needs to be able to develop fully and remain in a state of balance to function healthily. When we have mental and emotional problems with the central issues of each chakra this creates an imbalance in the chakra which can affect the physical nature causing ill health. Below is a description of the seven chakras.

The Seven Chakras

The base chakra is located at the base of the spine and is also called the root chakra. This chakra is coloured red and the central issue connected to this chakra is survival, its goal is to keep us safe and grounded in the physical world. It contains our will to live life enthusiastically and our wellbeing. On a physical level the base chakra deals with our excretory system and blood distribution.

The next chakra is the sacral plexus which is located in the lower stomach and is coloured orange and the central issue connected to this chakra is our sexuality, emotions and desire, it contains our creative spark and in-built talents. On a physical level the sacral plexus chakra deals with our reproductive system.

The next chakra is the solar plexus which is located just above the naval and is coloured yellow and the central issue connected to this chakra is the formation of our will power, inner strength and confidence to be a powerful creative and independent person. On a physical level the solar plexus chakra deals with our digestive system.

The next chakra is the heart chakra which is located near the heart area and is coloured a beautiful soft green with a pink centre. The central issue connected to this chakra is the expressing of our emotions and feelings and the ability to live from an open heart. Love and relationships are also central issues with this chakra along with self-acceptance. It is the bridge that connects the lower chakras to the upper chakras and is the seat of our soul. When the heart chakra is open it automatically helps with the healthy functioning of the other chakras. Balance and giving and receiving love is centred here. On a physical level the heart chakra deals with the immune system.

The next chakra is the throat chakra and is located in the throat and is coloured turquoise blue. The central issue connected to this chakra is communication and self-expression. It helps us to live our truth from a path of the heart not the head. We can also teach from a point of truth when we teach that which we have experienced and overcome. On a physical level the throat chakra deals with the thyroid.

The next chakra is the third eye chakra and is located between the eyebrows and is coloured a deep indigo. The central issue connected to this chakra is with our intuition and imagination we can develop this chakra to see clearly from a spiritual point of view. This is the clairvoyant centre and we can receive visual images from our imagination to interpret as actual or symbolic meanings for ourselves or others. On a physical level the third eye chakra deals the pituitary gland and the central nervous system.

The final chakra is the crown chakra and is located at the top of the head. The colour is violet and the central issue connected to this chakra is our spirituality and unity with the Divine. It is our spiritual alignment to our source energy, our guides, angels and higher self. We have awareness and wisdom when we fully develop this chakra. On a physical level the crown chakra deals with the pineal gland and upper brain.

To remember the colours of the chakras in order, my spiritual teachers taught me this saying: 'Richard Of York Gave Battle In Vain', giving you the initial of each chakra colour.

We can visualize opening the chakras by seeing them spinning and filled with light. We can also with intent make them as vibrant as possible topping them up with their own associated colour. It is wise to constantly clean our chakras with light and visualization exercises as they can become clogged and overloaded with psychic debris. You can do this in the same way that you do the grounding exercise from chapter one but instead focus on each chakra and imagine any negative energy leaving each one from the crown to the base and draining down the cord into the centre of the Earth to be neutralized. Once this is done top up the colour of your chakra with either white light or its own colour. You will be helping to keep your chakras balanced and in good working order, which in turn helps you in your psychic work.

Colour Vibrations

Now that you have information on each chakra, you are preparing your vibes through knowledge and wisdom as psychic development requires theory as well as practical work. Next we will take a deeper look into colour interpretations to show you how each colour vibration represents each chakra and their central issues. Reading the colours expressed within the aura and chakras, is what will help you to be able to accurately read the vibes. I have an easy method for you to begin your first aura reading on someone and that is through using coloured ribbons. You can pick up these coloured ribbons at a local craft shop or market stall, make sure you have picked out all the colours of the chakras and any others that take your fancy. These ribbons will become the foundation of gaining valuable information in your aura readings building confidence in your abilities. Eventually this will help you to fine tune your psychic ability to such a degree it will become automatic to your senses.

You may receive colour images that just pop in your mind when you tune into the energy field of another after much practice with the ribbons. You will also become aware of a 'just knowing or sensing vibe' through your intuition with how you receive colours. By understanding the language of colours, you gain a great depth of information about a person from the state of their health along with relationship issues, their career, their finances, their dreams and desires as well as their personality. The following exercise will help to activate clairvoyance as well as strengthening the intuitive part of your soul. I have set the colours out in such a way where by it is easier for you understand. Read through the colours first before you do the exercise at the end. I have included enough information to get you started but you must use your vibes to add to your psychic alphabet and build on the information already given.

The Red Ribbon
If someone has picked the red ribbon then you will find the following vibes may fit their present circumstances.

Health Vibes: They may be due for blood tests, may have

circulation problems and blood problems. They may have problems with body temperature (cold feet), problems with the lower back at the base of the spine, the hips, the legs and the feet. They can also have pain and swelling in these areas.

Money Vibes: They may be about to buy property, move house or build their own home. They could be about to change their job, retire, sort out pensions, life insurances or financial investments and savings.

Relationship Vibes: They may be lacking chemistry and passion in their relationship.

Personality Vibes: They can be ambitious and enthusiastic, determined and courageous. They can also be the opposite and lack any drive and enthusiasm to move forward in life. They can be fiery, easily angered, stubborn and five sensory. Interpret as you feel.

Career Vibes: Any career that will be connected with the security of the material world, financial institutions like banks, insurances firms. I have come across those who work with blood such as nurses and forensic scientists, and those who build and design for a living creating security for others, builders and architects. The armed forces can be attached to this colour as their job is to survive and keep our country safe and secure.

The Orange Ribbon
If someone has picked the orange ribbon then you will find the following vibes may fit their present circumstances.

Health Vibes: They may have women's issues with the reproductive organs, prostrate problems in men, they may be pregnant or trying for a baby, have had a miscarriage or abortion.

They could have problems with their bowels, kidneys and lower stomach. They may be experiencing depression or grieving from some kind of loss.

Money Vibes: They can be very creative with great ideas and inspiration to make their own money through their own unique skills.

Relationship Vibes: They may be in the early stages of a new relationship or healing within an existing relationship and having a new start.

Personality Vibes: They are creative and eager and full of new ideas and inspiration to make things happen. Can sometimes come across as naïve and too eager to make decisions that may not be in their best interests. They are touchy feely and express their feelings outwardly. They may be interested in health and fitness and enjoy doing things that involve creative expression like dancing and yoga.

Career Vibes: Any career that can involve using one's creative energy, like artists, designers, poets. They may also choose acting and drama. As they are creative they are likely to choose ways in which to make their own money which usually means they will be self-employed.

The Yellow Ribbon
If someone has picked the yellow ribbon then you will find the following vibes may fit their present circumstances.

Health Vibes: They may have stomach problems, digestive complaints, diabetes, anorexia or bulimia, diarrhoea, nervous anxiety and depression or lack of spark.

Money Vibes: They may make their money from being in a powerful leading position and do what they can to get to the top to earn the big bucks along with the enjoyment of power.

Relationship Vibes: They may be about to get married or form some kind of commitment after finding happiness and fulfilment with their loved one.

Yellow Personality: They are powerful and strong characters and enjoy learning and are intelligent. They love to read, they are filled with positive intentions to make things happen, they rely on their gut instinct, they are generally happy with a sunny personality. Again all of this can be reversed you need to trust your vibes to see what you are feeling.

Career Vibes: Any career that can be connected with intuitive hunches, like the police force, fire service, bounty hunters and psychics. They may also choose a leading position like the head of a company, a director, a politician. The sunny personalities of this colour can also produce great actors and comedians who love to make people laugh.

The Green Ribbon

If someone has picked the green ribbon then you will find the following vibes may fit their present circumstances.

Health Vibes: They may have asthma, lung disease, heart palpitations or cardiac disease, problems with blood pressure and colds, and also problems with self-worth and self-acceptance.

Money Vibes: They may make their money from heart centred careers and will often do volunteer and charity work. They feel that they like to give a lot, even if it is their own time spent and so may not make as much money as they need to live.

Relationship Vibes: They can be completely settled in a long and happy marriage or relationship with a growing family or they can be at the stage in life where by the love for their partner is more like a sibling love and not a passionate love. This is why marriages can break up after 25 years of happiness. Use your vibes to see how you feel.

Personality Vibes: They are very caring and giving but this can be to the detriment of their health. They may struggle with balance and always be running late as they often put others' needs before their own. They can be too nice and so easily walked over therefore they can be fatigued, drained of energy and will need to set boundaries.

Career Vibes: Any career that can be connected to the heart, unconditional love and healing. Nurses, medical profession, parents, charity work, healers, mediums and psychics.

The Pink Ribbon
If someone has picked the pink ribbon then you will find the following vibes may fit their present circumstances.

Health Vibes: They may have the same health problems as the green ribbon as they both belong to the same chakra.

Money Vibes: Again look to the green ribbon.

Relationship Vibes: Usually if someone has picked this colour, they have either fallen madly in love and want to know if things are going to work out for them, or they have just broken up with their loved one and are broken hearted.

Pink Personality: They are a very sensitive soul and words can hurt them deeply. They can forgive but not forget and they worry about things before they have happened. They have good imaginations and often follow their hearts ignoring their egos and head. They fall in love easily and need to feel special in a relationship. They love to feel feminine and enjoy surrounding themselves with things that help them to feel this way. They can cry when they watch sad films or read negative stories in the media and worry about the violence in the world.

Career Vibes: Psychics and healers are very heart centred and sensitive. Other careers that belong to this colour are veterinarians, animal workers, health workers, medical profession, singers, actors, dancers and anything that requires a sensitive quality.

The Turquoise Ribbon
If someone has picked the turquoise ribbon then you will find the following vibes may fit their present circumstances.

Health Vibes: They may have throat problems, thyroid problems, neck and shoulder problems, mouth, nose and ear problems. The arms and hands can also be affected with health problems. They may have problems communicating with the self – heart over head or have problems communicating with others.

Money Vibes: They may make their money through their own creative skills just like the orange colour as both are creative. They can literally put their money where their mouth is and earn their finances through their communication skills.

Relationship Vibes: They can be in a relationship where there is a communication breakdown and they are just going through the motions without talking over their problems. They can also be in a controlling relationship if one is more verbal than the other. They can be in a balanced loving relationship where by both partners communicate their needs equally. Again use your vibes.

Personality Vibes: They are verbal and express their needs and wants without fear of upset or offence. They cannot go too long without letting someone know that they have upset them, as they are used to talking things through and not keeping it inside.

Career Vibes: They make great teachers, lectures or any job where communicative skills are needed. Blue is also the colour of healing along with green and so healers and the medical profession can also belong to this colour.

The Indigo Ribbon

If someone has picked the indigo ribbon then you will find the following vibes may fit their present circumstances.

Health Vibes: They may have eye problems, sleep problems, nightmares and headaches. They can have problems making decisions and become clouded in their thinking making them become out of touch with reality. They may experience problems with their memory.

Money Vibes: They will use their intellect and wisdom to make their money. They rely on their intuition and feelings to help others or themselves in their career.

Relationship Vibes: They can be in a successful relationship where they can see themselves growing old with their loved one. They also rely on the way they feel in a relationship and listen to their intuition to know they are doing the right thing.

Personality Vibes: They are visionaries and have amazing imaginations; they are great story tellers and have a wonderful charismatic aura. On the other hand, they can come across as day dreamers or out of touch with reality if not grounded.

Career Vibes: They make excellent psychics, mediums and healers. They also make great scientists as they need to be focussed, open minded and have a great intellect. They can be inventors and writers and in any job that requires inspiration and vision.

The Violet Ribbon

If someone has picked the violet ribbon then you will find the following vibes may fit their present circumstances.

Health Vibes: They can have problems with coordination when off balance along with confusion and mental problems. Depression can also set in when there is an imbalance between the left and right sides of the brain.

Money Vibes: They can usually put their hands to anything to make their money as they are open minded, intelligent and wise, have life experience. They do the work they love instead of just taking any job, making them happy and fulfilled. They are in touch with their destiny and know what path to follow.

Relationship Vibes: They can be in a soul mate relationship with someone who is totally on their wavelength. They are six sensory and will only attract six sensory partners to them.

Personality Vibes: They are charming, wise, intelligent, inspirational, creative and wonderful natural leaders. You feel uplifted to be in their company. They set a good example and live their truth at all times taking responsibility for their lives. They are six sensory.

Career Vibes: They make wonderful philosophers, poets, guides in life, mediums, healers, religious leaders or have any important roles that reach a lot of people to inspire them.

Exercise to Read the Ribbons

Find someone willing to have a reading. Do your tuning in exercise from chapter one and white light yourself. Remember that I have given you a guideline with the colour interpretations but there are many more than I have included here and so you need to use your intuition along with your psychic senses when reading the ribbons. You will find that if you do this then you will come across new information to add to your journal of vibes. With every reading you do you will come to understand the pattern of information received in connection to the ribbons and soon you will become natural in your psychic style. For every meaning of each colour you can also reverse the positive to the negative if you feel this may be the case, these will then become blocks in the client's life.

- Ask your client to pick their favourite colour from the ribbons – this will represent what is on their mind as well as their personality. Example – if the colour is red, they will have financial issues on their mind, they may be about to have a blood test. Their personality may be five sensory and sceptical or they can be ambitious and determined in their out look.

- Ask your client to pick the colour that they are drawn too – this will represent certain aspects they need to address in their present circumstances. Example – if the colour is orange, they may have inner depression or grief from a loss of some kind. They may be drawn to starting a family and desire to get pregnant. They may need to pay attention to their dreams and desires to create fulfilment within their lives.

- Ask your client to pick the colour they dislike or their least favourite colour if they like them all – this will represent the blocks they have in their life and you can help them to discover what they need to work through. Example – if the colour is pink, they may be heart broken and need to address relationship issues because it is affecting all other parts of their life. They may need to learn to love and approve of themselves first to be able to attract the love they desire.

Finish the exercise, cleanse with light, tune out and close down.

Now you need to get feedback from your client to see how well you have done. You will discover you scored some hits and if not direct ones then you will have hit on the essence of the subject. You can also learn through having feedback from your client what you have missed out on with the ribbons. Notice this and remember them for when reading another client. I have only given you three questions you can use your creative side and make your own questions up, see what works best for you. Usually when someone picks out the three colours you will have an overall awareness of everything you need to say about their lives, covering their health, relationships, finances, career and personality.

Now a quick look, at what colour vibrations can do for you:

Wear red if you are tired and need an extra energy boost.
Wear orange if you are depressed or stuck in your creativity.
Wear yellow if your spark has gone and you need to feel uplifted.
Wear green if you need space to balance your emotions.
Wear pink to help you with issues of self-love.
Wear blue to calm you down and be able to communicate clearly.
Wear indigo to help you with your intuitive ability.

Wear violet to connect you to spiritual awareness and be inspired to fulfil your destiny.

Vibes Check List

- Use your intuition and the psychic senses along with the colour interpretations to receive a well rounded accurate psychic reading.

- Further your psychic studies with extra information on the aura and chakras.

- Practice makes perfect, make sure you always get feedback from your client and still notice when you may be wrong so you can gain a deeper awareness of the colours.

- Experiment with wearing different colours to see how they react with you and make you feel. You will then come to understand the colours of the soul.

CHAPTER FOUR

Vibe the Future

Predicting the future is what psychics are mostly known for and expected to do – although you already know that other parts of a psychic reading are far more important than just giving predictions. A true psychic is there to help the person to heal their own life and inspire them to use their own intuition to help themselves along their path. By touching the soul of the person you help them to understand their own divinity. Some people get excited at the prospect of visiting a psychic to find out what will happen to them in their future, they have no understanding that the future is in their own hands or the part that they play in unfolding it. They are sadly lacking in awareness of the fact that they are the master of their own ship and are creating their future already, although unaware and by default. The wise and professional psychic will inform their clients that only certain things in their future are set in stone but everything else is the result of their own free will. This means they create a huge part of the future themselves and need to take responsibility for creating their dreams and desires and for ridding themselves of all the mess. I love the saying, stop waiting and start creating I have repeated this statement to many. The point of power is always in the present moment and that power is called change.

The Role of a Psychic

Predicting the future may not be the most important part of psychic work but it can be the most exciting part. I know that some people will conjure up the image of a psychic, dressed in a head scarf complete with a crystal ball and ready to predict their fortune. Those days have long gone and now you will find reputable psychics dressed in business suits in their own office with their own staff. The public opinion of psychics is changing and psychics with good reputations are now gaining public acclaim for their work, especially since the media have produced psychic shows and television dramas that reach millions of people. A psychic's role is to offer guidance on the client's life path for their highest good. They can make the client aware of any lessons and obstacles that are causing them pain and upset in their life that they may be choosing to ignore or bury. These are called psychic blocks and are a part of our destiny to overcome and master. If we face our blocks and deal with them, then we may experience temporary pain and upset but soon the clouds will clear and the weight will fall off our shoulders and we will experience the happiness we thought couldn't happen.

Psychic Reflections

Usually when someone seeks psychic guidance they want to make changes in their life and are looking for reassurance to double check that they are doing the right thing. Most people know what they want to do, like changing jobs, moving house or getting married and so they want to check if their decisions are wise and will turn out successful. They sub-consciously fear trusting their own decisions in case they fail and so they ignore their own intuitive nature and choose to visit a psychic. They hope that the psychic will give them the good news they are after and be told they are going to be wealthy, healthy and happy in their future. A reputable psychic will give them guidance based on the clients present circumstances that offer the direction their life will unfold in if decisions are taken or if they decide to remain as they are.

The present moment is the moment that needs to be altered for the future to flow in the way you desire it. Psychics act like a mirror for the person to look into and see what they need to make their lives work. The psychic reflects back to them all that they need via

70

the clients own aura and vibes. The answers are already within them as everyone is already psychic and has the gift of intuition.

The reason I teach psychic vibes development throughout the world, is to help others know how to use and trust in their vibes so they can enhance their lives and live in fulfilment with peace of mind, instead of worry and fear of the future. I also want to help as many people as I can to realize they have a soul and are eternal.

Psychic Guidance

I have a waiting list of clients wanting a psychic reading for help and guidance in their life, and my intention is to help my clients in such a way that they will not need any more psychic guidance in the future unless they are stuck. To be fair, we all need help sometimes in our life and there are many other sources of help available out there in the world for us, so we will be drawn in a certain direction. What I discourage are people who are constantly seeking the advice of a psychic because they do not want to take responsibility for their life and this is a very unhealthy state to be in. They will have self-esteem issues and lack confidence and want to keep coming back for reassurance. Also one psychic won't be enough for them and they can become addicted to visiting several, they waste their money as they search for the prediction that all is going to work out for them without any participation on their part. This is never going to happen they are deluding themselves, they think I can wave a magic wand over their heads and make things instantly better. Part of our life purpose is to learn how to create our own lives with the free will that God gave us and we all have this power of creation to do the best we can with it.

Psychic guidance is a valuable tool, to help the client become encouraged to improve their circumstances. It is the free will of the client to follow this advice or not. A psychic should never make decisions for you or insist that you make them. This does not serve growth and takes the clients power away to choose for themselves. Psychics are not there to save or heal the client themselves and if they think they are then this is their ego talking. Psychic guidance is given to help the client be able to save and heal themselves. This will then stop the psychic from interfering with the karma and spiritual growth of the client and incurring karma themselves. Healing can only begin when the person is ready to heal, until this time comes, nothing will happen.

Past, Present and Future

A psychic can bring you to a place in the present moment, explaining to you why your life is the way it is because of your previous life choices. This helps you to understand the consequences of your actions. The past, present and future are all linked together, as one affects the other and because of this time line predictions are able to be made. If you hold onto the pain and upset of the past, it will continue to upset you in the present moment and what you are feeling today is creating your tomorrows. This is you becoming stuck in the patterns of the past and without an effort to change things these patterns will keep on repeating themselves causing accurate predictable outcomes.

Throughout your life you will be presented with opportunities that require you to make changes. It is your free will to go for these opportunities or to let them pass you by. When a psychic looks into the future all they see are probabilities based on the way your life is flowing along with possibilities of change through new opportunities. This is why predictions cannot always be spot on accurate, as clients can change their mind at the last minute and not take the chances that present themselves.

Written in Stone

We are born with a blueprint which is known as our destiny. It is what we have agreed to do, learn and experience during our incarnation on Earth. These are known as our life lessons. You choose the life you were born into and sometimes this can be hard for our conscious mind to accept, especially if we have had painful lives filled with trauma, abuse, poverty and illness. This original pathway is fixed and written in stone, we chose it to perfect our soul through spiritual growth and understanding.

Sometimes a psychic is unable to predict the arrival of a lesson, purely because it may not be in the best interests of the client. This will be determined by the guides and angels of the client, for they are aware of the bigger picture and if it is not for the highest good of the client, the information will be blocked from the psychic. The reason being, if they receive news that they are about to experience a traumatic event, this will cause them unease and fear and they may try to make drastic unwise choices to see if they can advert it even though they can't.

However, there are times when the psychic will be able to offer them guidance on the stress that is about to unfold in their life as this can give them the encouragement to work through it. A week before I broke my leg I was in the middle of a meditation and was told by my guide that things were about to become quite stressful and I was to stay strong and calm and all would be well. I had no idea what was about to happen but felt reassured that my guide knew and offered me the best advice for my problem. It was only six weeks to my wedding day and I thought that the stress coming may be connected to the plans. A week later I slipped on the stairs, broke my leg and ankle and ended up in plaster up to my knee. I considered postponing my wedding but had an inner feeling and reassurance that I would come through it all right. I had to have an operation on my leg and had ten pins and three plates put in it and the surgeon was doubtful that the plaster would come off in time. I would not be able to fly to my honeymoon in New York if the plaster stayed on. All this extra stress on top of preparing for my wedding could have lead me to postponing the day and cancelling my honeymoon. I decided to stay strong and remain calm as my guide suggested and ended up healing a lot quicker than was expected, my plaster came off two days before my wedding day and I walked down the aisle on crutches and two days later set off on my honeymoon.

As a professional psychic, you have to be responsible for what comes out of your mouth and you should always work in the name of the light. Apart from the things that are written in stone, free will is then used to live our life in the way we decide to react to things. It is not the lesson that is so much important, it is how we react and overcome the obstacle in our path that really matters. This determines whether or not we stay stuck in our life and play the victim card or if we learn from it move forward and have the experience put firmly behind us. Through this we are able to help others who are newly experiencing what we have just overcome. There are ways for us to look into the future to gain the information we need so we can alter our current path or be prepared for wonderful opportunities.

Divination

There are tools that you can use to help you divine or predict the future. Such tools are things like the tarot cards, the rune stones, the crystal ball and dousing. Using these tools can give you confidence in your psychic work, along with strengthening your intuition. I am also going to show you a way to tap into the future without using any tools other than your own mind. Personally I have an affinity with the tarot cards and have found over the last ten years of using them to be an accurate predictive tool along with offering great insights into a person's state of mind and life lessons. Tarot cards can also help you to develop clairvoyance, as the pictures of each card unlock symbolic information held deep within the subconscious mind. I will be writing a book on understanding the tarot in the near future to help budding psychics unfold their sixth sense. If you are going to use any tools for divination it is wise to try a few different kinds to find the one that best suits you.

Tarot Predictions for Two Clients

A client was trying for a baby and was having no luck in getting pregnant. She came for a tarot reading and the cards revealed her desires for a baby in her present circumstances and also information about the problem that was causing her problems in conceiving. She had to let go of her inner fears about being able to properly care for her child and change her thoughts to be more positive. If she did this the tarot cards showed that in eight weeks time she would be pregnant. I am pleased to say that's exactly what happened and eight weeks later my client phoned me up to let me know the wonderful news, she had conceived.

Another client came for a reading to ask me if their marriage was going to survive. After I looked into the cards showing me the present moment they revealed my client was having an affair with someone else. I looked ahead into the future and could see that if this affair carried on within two months her husband would find out and leave her. She now had the free will to alter this by giving up her lover but I am sad to say this did not happen and two months later her husband was tipped off and caught them in the act. They are now divorced.

I am now going to show you how to tune into the future without the use of any tools. You need to record any information you get in your journal as it has not happened yet. By doing this you can check back on your accuracy along with noticing any free will decisions that were made that altered the outcome. You are going to practice on yourself first and then on a friend before you progress to clients.

Exercise to Predict the Future

Do the Tuning In exercise from chapter one and surround yourself with white light.

Get comfortable and ready to begin.

Now you need to use your imagination and visualization skills to perform this exercise. Focus your mind in the here and now, the present.

Imagine you are connected to a time line and you are able to move back and forwards at will. At this moment you are in the present but now I am going to ask you to go backwards in time to an age that holds very happy memories.

Now you are in the past, actually feel what it is like to be living the memories of the past as if you are consciously back there now.

Now bring yourself back to the present moment in time and feel your awareness in the here and now.

Now it is time to go forward in time, only one day ahead, you do this by going through your usual morning routine in your imagination along with stating your intent that it is the following day in your mind.

Now as you float through your day in your imagination it is time to notice anything that stands out to you that is unusual or unexpected.

Maybe you notice someone you haven't seen in a while, maybe you hear parts of a conversation not yet spoken and maybe you see yourself being somewhere you haven't planned on going. Use all of your psychic senses to obtain information.

Once you are satisfied you have enough information bring your awareness back to the present day. Do the Tuning Out exercise and white light yourself.

Well done, you have just completed your first future forecast. If you find it easier to start with a blank screen instead of imagining the beginning of your new day then all you need do is use your visualization skills to imagine a cinema screen or a blank wall.

This will help you to clear and focus your mind for receiving random images and information without you assuming you are making it all up. Both ways work well but you do need to stretch yourself and try both a good few times. If you find you would prefer to create a blackboard or a television screen then try those, you will soon notice one that seems to work best for you. If you get stuck and think your imagination is getting in the way then all you need to do is clear your screen and start afresh. You will then have a fresh canvas to paint your work of art.

The goal is not to go too far ahead into the future as the further you go the predictions get trickier as free will can play a huge part in altering things. It is a great idea to practice this exercise often as you will get stronger and become more accurate with every try. Don't worry if you do not seem to be adept at reading the future in this way – there are other avenues to use for divination. When I give psychic readings I usually look at the next three months of a client's life using this exercise or if asked certain specific questions I use the tarot cards to look further ahead. You can keep stretching for more information a month at a time and record your predictions for later review.

People who are excellent at reading the future in this way can go on to develop remote viewing. There are psychics who have been tested by scientists in remote viewing and some are used by the government for top secret projects, The Star Gate Project was one and to find out more about this you can read my husbands book called 'Powers of the Sixth Sense' published by O Books. Psychics are also able to use remote viewing to link in with missing persons and crime investigations. It is the ability to see clearly within the mind and the development of clairvoyance in this way can be likened to short snippets of video recordings being played.

An example of looking into the Future

This is purely to show you that even though the information is of no particular use, the fact that I picked it up can help me to validate I was actually ahead in time. This can be a valuable tool to develop to help others for their highest good.

I decided to look one day ahead in my future because I had nothing planned the next day and was going to just go with the flow. This was great to use as an experiment as I had no assumptions of what my day would hold.

First thing I did was use a blank wall to clear and focus my mind ready to receive random images. Next I placed an intention in my mind that I was one day ahead in time and waited to receive images. I had a quick flash in my mind of a duck followed by her babies swimming slowly along the river bank. Again I cleared my mind, brought back the blank wall and received my next image of an old fashioned red phone box. Once more I cleared my mind and this time had an image of cheese and wine on a tray. I decided to go one step further and find out what the cheese and wine meant and then had an image of an art gallery.

The Results

Next day my husband and I decided to take a run in the car, we stopped near a river and I got out and walked to the edge and at that moment a duck and her ducklings floated past. Later that afternoon my husband received a call about his photographs, he is a keen photographer. This person owned an art gallery and suggested to my husband that he could show his work off at a cheese and wine evening. About the red phone box... well, I came across that week's later on a trip into the Highlands of Scotland. Maybe that was a free will thing or my mind wandered further ahead in time. At the end of the day two out of three isn't bad and it was a great experiment – and that's what you also need to do, experiment with your vibes.

Predictive Practice Exercise

Here are some ways that you can practice this predictive practice exercise:

- Weather predictions, psychics have been known to predict snow fall in hot countries
- The headlines of the following day's newspapers
- The next President to be elected
- The winner of a competition like dancing with the stars
- The marriage of a celebrity or the break up of one
- A pregnancy

Remember you may not get direct hits but you can get snippets of the bigger picture. Keep recording your predictions and notice when those snippets become stronger eventually turning into direct hits. The best way to develop your divinations skills is through meditation as this helps to still the mind, freeing it to act as a receptor receiving information from the future.

Meditation

Relaxation and meditation is one of the best ways to enhance your psychic vibes to strengthen them and gain success when using them. Just a few minutes each day to begin with, will be of great benefit in developing your psychic senses, encouraging them to the surface and into your conscious awareness. Meditation will also prove to be of positive benefit for your health reducing stress, blood pressure and worry. Daily meditation can help you to become more focused in your life, helping you to make clearer decisions. When you still your mind from the clutter of daily stresses and strains, you move from a world of harsh vibrations to a world of inner peace and quiet. Meditation is the time where you become at one with your soul and tap into the divine power of the universe. When this happens you are in a state of harmony and balance and are in the right frame of mind to help manifest your dreams and desires. We will explore this in a later chapter, on using your vibes to manifest success.

Here are two different ways in which to meditate, one method will help to develop your intuition and sensitivity to your guides and angels, and the other to develop and strengthen your clairvoyance, helping you with accuracy in your visions and predictions.

For either meditation, you need to be able to find a place that you feel happy and comfortable with, where you will not be disturbed. I do mine in the morning when I awake and before I start my day. Simply ask your guide and angel to protect you and imagine or visualize the white light of the Holy Spirit surrounding you. Remember the importance of protection is to protect yourself from unwanted energies that may have a negative or adverse effect on your emotions and physical health.

You are also stating your belief in a divine power and universal energy that fills your spirit, making your existence possible. Protection is the intention of focussing towards the light and staying away from negative or lower vibrations that may wish to meddle with you. If you are fearful for any reason, then do not bother with meditation until you feel you are in a more secure state of mind. Daily meditation will speed up your psychic development and you will soon notice the difference. You will also discover that you end up meditating for longer periods of time than when you first started, and this happens naturally.

Meditation for Sensitivity

First make sure there are no noisy interruptions around you. Close your eyes and feel yourself relaxing from your head to your toes. The quickest way to do this is give a couple of deep sighs and let your shoulders drop and loosen. Concentrate on your breathing for a few moments counting or noticing your breaths in and out.

You may soon be aware of seeing colours within your mind, if so you can move on to noticing these colours. If you feel neither of these are any good for you then you can choose a special thought or affirmation so that you can give it your full attention. When doing this, you are training your mind to focus and concentrate, refusing to acknowledge the clutter of useless thoughts that play out. Daily practice will help to clear the mind and create a space, for you to notice the psychic impressions when they appear there. Eventually the goal of this type of meditation is to find that you no longer need to focus on anything to attain the goal of stillness. This is not as easy as it may sound but with practice you can build up to longer periods of time of inner stillness before your mind wanders again.

By using this form of meditation, you will notice within weeks that you are more able to concentrate and focus on situations in your life without losing patience or becoming irritable. You will also find that you become more in tune with your intuition and psychic senses, because you have created a space for them to be revealed.

Meditation for Clairvoyance
For speeding up the development of clairvoyance a visualization meditation is a great tool as it conjures up vivid mental images and pictures within your mind. I get my students to listen to a guided tape or to my voice as I take them on a journey encouraging them to see and feel by using visualization and imagination. Imagination is the bridge to self awareness and the power of the mind is mighty. Again make sure there are no noisy interruptions around you. Relax and ask for protection.

Next I want you to imagine that you are leaving your home and closing the door behind you. See all of this as vividly in your mind as you can, taking time to notice what is familiar to you. This will help to kick start your imagination through memory. Once the door is closed, imagine stepping into a beautiful meadow and fill it with exactly what you want to see there, maybe you want rows of olive trees or fields of flowers. This is your time to create your work of art and make your meadow as beautiful as you like, is it sunny and warm or do you prefer it cool, frosty or snowy?

It is your imagination so make it perfect for you. When you decide to leave the meadow you just need walk back to your door, go through it and close it behind you. Bring your awareness back into your room and open your eyes. By using this form of meditation you will notice that your clairvoyant ability will strengthen helping you when you need to predict or see actual or symbolic information. You may also be aware when doing this exercise that you can smell different smells and even have a sensation of tasting something. If you find this to be the case for you, then you may end up using these skills when conducting psychic readings for others.

Once you have completed your meditations, say thank you for the protection given, white light yourself and ground your energy with a drink or snack.

With the visualization meditation you can change your destination and visit new scenery as your imagination is limitless. You can also use this meditation to meet with your guides and angels. If you are ready they visit with you in your meadow and you may receive their names or spiritual guidance from them. The key is to experiment with what you have learned and be creative to find out what works best for you.

Vibes Check List

• Remember that the past, present and future all belong as one. To change the future you must let go of the hurt in the past and not be affected in the present moment.

• Know that you have certain things set in stone in your life called your destiny the rest is created by the use of your free will.

- If working on clients, be responsible for what comes out of your mouth. Never tell someone what to do or cause them to feel fear and unease.

- Check out divination tools to find which one works best for you. Tarot cards are great for predictions.

- When looking into the future you either see probabilities of what will happen or possibilities of what may happen.

- Practice your predictions with the power of your own mind. Use the suggestions for things to practice on.

- Learn to meditate both for sensitivity and clairvoyance.

- Remember to always white light yourself and ask for protection when doing any psychic work.

CHAPTER FIVE

Mediumship

Now you are going to explore how mediumship works and also receive information on the spirit world and its inhabitants. Mediumship is a natural progression after exploring and developing your psychic side. Mediumship is a skill that can be developed by anyone who has the commitment, desire and a correct attitude in wanting to use it. The spirit world knows if you are committed and have the best intentions and based on this will determine the unfolding of your innate mediumistic abilities. Your own vibration will attract you to develop this skill – five sensory people will not be bothered about developing their mediumship. Some mediums say that not all psychics are mediums but all mediums are psychic. I know of psychics who are brilliant mediums and I know of mediums that have no real understanding of their own psychic nature. We all have the same soul gifts so if anyone is determined enough to want to develop the gift of mediumship in this life time then they will be able to do so to their own unique level. The difference being, some mediums are stronger and more natural than others, in the same way as some of us find playing a musical instrument, singing or dancing, easier than others do. Mediums that are more natural will have an affinity with this skill and find understanding the language of the spirit world easier to decipher than others may, they may have also been aware of unusual occurrences in childhood. Such mediums can be used to reach more people in this world as part of their destiny to help us receive the message of life continuing on after death. John Edward the New York medium from the hit television series Crossing Over has accomplished this. My good friend Terry has seen him appear live in London and she commented on how naturally and accurately his mediumship flowed in front of such a large crowd. She also said he could put his shoes under her bed anytime, I wonder what she could mean! Now the first thing you need to understand is the different roles between psychics and mediums.

Psychics

Psychics can feel and tune into subtle energy vibrations of people through their auras and also absorb residual energy from places and objects to gain information. Once they have a psychic link with someone, they can use their vibes to sense and gain accurate information on the true character of the person, bypassing the personality or ego that is shown to others. Psychics can tune into the timeline of the past and present conditions of their client, to be able to give probable predictions for the future. They also see possibilities of change in the future through opportunistic events and explain to the client it is their free will to take advantage of this change or not. An advanced psychic will help their client become aware of the need to take responsibility for their life by listening to their intuition and using their free will for the highest good. They participate in changing their own life rather than sitting on the fence and waiting for change to happen.

When sensing and reading someone's aura they are also able to pick up on the state of health and balance of the individual often revealing current ongoing health problems, medical checkups or even early warnings of an illness that has yet developed in the physical body. Another important role a psychic plays is being able to tune into a persons life lessons and destiny as this is contained within their aura. Psychics can read the chakras revealing any emotional blockages that are holding the person back and giving psychic guidance on how to heal through them. A strong and balanced psychic is extremely aware of their surroundings and use their vibes consciously and consistently at all times, especially when they encounter any new situation or person along their path. This not only gives them the power to make wiser life choices but also helps them to be protected and safe. They trust their intuition and listen to what the heart is feeling about any given influence. Finally a psychic will tune into their sixth sense by placing their intent, focus and attention on the person, place or object they desire to read, this creates a psychic link to receive the information.

Mediums

Mediums are channels for the spirit world to communicate through to connect with people still alive on the earth plane. Mediums have fine tuned their senses and have the ability to be able to see, hear and sense what the spirit wishes to impart to others. Just like a telephone helps two individuals to connect and talk with each other over a distance, a medium acts like a receiver and then transmits the information to the person being given the message. A true medium will provide evidence of the continuance of life after death by bringing through enough information from the spirit, so their loved ones on earth can recognize them. Evidence may include things like how they passed? It could be from an illness or an accident or they may have passed away at home or in the hospital, a medium will be able to tell. Other kinds of evidence a medium will pass on, are descriptions of what the spirit person looked like when alive, for instance, they may have been very tall, short, large or small, they may have had distinguishing marks on their bodies or specific tattoos.

Mediums could also describe the spirit communicators hair colour and style when alive, the colour of their eyes, whether they wore glasses or not, the list is pretty endless. Other important kinds of evidence include the character, personality and age of the spirit when passing along with specific names connected in their family or if possible their own name and 'who they are' – mum or dad, sister or brother, grandparent, family or friend. Also important dates that mark special or specific events and provide evidence from spirit are anniversaries of passings, birthdays or weddings along with wonderful memories once shared and never forgotten. All of this evidence will help the loved one on earth to recognize their loved one in the spirit world. If a medium fails to communicate any of the above, then they are probably reading the aura from the person having the reading and working psychically instead. When developing your mediumship, this is the kind of evidence that you should be aspiring to bring through.

Sceptics

Sceptics or as I call them septics, only joking, often think that mediumship is just an amusing and entertaining parlour trick or that the medium is using their psychic ability to obtain information about the so-called spirit from the client's aura. Obviously information about any person that has shared their history with us can be found within our aura. This is because the aura is our own individual Akashik record of everything that has ever been, said and done, including all relationships. A medium can easily slip from spirit contact and begin to tune into and read from the aura instead, you will notice this through them focussing on the client rather than giving evidence from the spirit. Mediums have quietened the sceptics by bringing through information from the spirit communicator that the client had no prior knowledge of. An example of this happened to my husband and I. Two psychic mediums living and working together can sometimes have its advantages for passing on messages from the spirit world. As we both know each other extremely well, we have to be sure we are not reading from each other's auras or picking up on things that have been subconsciously remembered from our past discussions. It is much easier to read for someone who you do not know and have no prior assumptions for.

Jock's father, whom I never got to meet, has passed on, and now and again he takes a chance to pop in and say hello quite unexpectedly. One such time he made his presence known to me and wanted me to pass a message on to Jock. I passed on a few things that Jock was able to validate and then his dad mentioned that soon he would receive some money from his grandmother's will. Now both Jock and I already knew that his grandmother had left no will and this was clarified by Jock's mother. Again Jock's dad repeated this information and as I have learned to trust in what spirit has to say I repeated the message back to Jock. I finished the rest of the impromptu reading and we both wondered what it all meant. Within two weeks Jock received a letter explaining that his grandmother had left a will that had recently been recovered and he would be receiving a small inheritance. This information was not known prior to the reading and therefore could not be gained from Jock's aura and goes to show that I was in direct contact and communication with the spirit of Jock's dad.

The Purpose of Mediumship

The main purpose of mediumship is to demonstrate the evidence of survival of the soul. In other words, the aim of mediumship is to show those on earth that there is life after death and when life on earth is over, a new adventure begins. Death is not final it is only death of the physical body that actually happens, our soul is released and our spirit moves to the next dimension and lives on. This understanding and knowledge can have tremendous results in how we choose to live our lives. Knowing that life continues and that we are accountable for our own souls growth, instils in us responsibility for our actions here and now. This understanding can help us to make a difference individually adding more peace within the world and ensuring spiritual growth. Five sensory people tend to ignore the possibility that there is life after death and sometimes they find themselves in a unique experience that opens their minds to fact that there is eternal life. These are called out-of-body or near death experiences.

Near Death Experiences

There have been instances where people have had near death experiences, they have literally died and gone back home to the spirit world and were given a choice to stay or to return back to life. On doing so they were inspired to change their lives and to show love and compassion to others, knowing at a deeper level that we are all linked. Some of these people were atheists and believed that when their time was up they would cease to exist. You can imagine the turn around within their lives when they discovered that – not only do they survive death but what they do with their lives on earth, actually matters. If you are interested in these fascinating real life stories, the book by Dr Raymond Moody called *Life After Life*, is an inspiring read.

Mediumship for Healing

The other obvious reason of mediumship is to help those who are still grieving and missing their loved ones and in this context, the use of mediumship can begin the healing process for those left behind. Often the spirit is willing the person to move through their grieving because they know that they have survived death and will reunite down the line once again. Grieving is a very personal thing that affects each person differently but the common thread is missing the physical contact. Mediumship can help with this by providing evidence to show that they have survived death and are alive and well in the spirit world. This can bring a deep inner peace to loved ones on earth who think they have lost them forever, especially if a child has passed before the parents, as this is often the saddest form of grief.

One other reason that I have come across during my work as a medium, is when spirit wishes to communicate to pass on advice or information about a problem, hard time or lesson that their loved one is currently experiencing. This helps to give them the encouragement and reassurance to get through this time, knowing they are receiving help from the other side. I have been told by the people receiving the messages they felt empowered to know that their loved ones are still aware of what is presently happening within their lives. This gives them the inner proof and knowing that they are still alive and well in spirit and that one day they will find each other again.

Just to clarify the most asked question I have come across through my work as a professional medium, No! Your loved ones do not watch you during intimate moments like your sex life or when you are on the toilet or with any other personal scenario. The spirit world has discretion and quite frankly has no interest in these matters that are private and personal to you.

The Motive of a Medium

The motive of a true medium is a spiritual one and the medium who has totally explored, studied and developed this immense purpose will know beyond a shadow of a doubt that mediumship is a process that serves the highest good of all humanity.

For this reason evolved teachers and masters in the spirit world can use a medium to channel and impart very important teachings and wisdom to us on earth to assist us all with our spiritual growth. They do this through what is known as trance, where by an evolved spirit uses the mediums body and mind to communicate spiritual teachings.

Also we have been blessed enough to have been shown the way, along with the truth of survival from death, from great spiritual teachers who have walked the Earth before us. Jesus Christ is a wonderful spiritual Master and teacher who came to earth and gave us spiritual knowledge and truths to better ourselves and humanity. These teachings carry on evolving from the other side and from time to time we are blessed with those special souls on earth who help to remind us of who we really are and how to evolve. We are here on earth for the purpose of progressing our souls and those of us who awaken to this truth, will be given the right teachings at the right time for our own individual level of vibration.

Messages that Heal

Mediumship can be used to bring immense peace and healing to both the spirit loved one and the loved one still alive. A medium is a bridge of love and works with the intention to heal the illusion of distance between spirits and those on earth. Many times when a loved one passes, those left behind feel that they never had a chance to say their goodbyes. This brings guilt and sorrow to the person grieving which in turn affects the loved one in spirit. Mediumship can be used to help bring closure to the pain felt at not being there during the dying process. There are also times when any unfinished business needs to be addressed to begin the healing process, for both parties. Regret about not saying the things that needed to be said or in sorting out any important issues when they had a chance, can keep both the spirit or loved one unable to move on. These can be issues of forgiveness or just needing to hear the words that they loved each other. It is a very tricky and sad situation, when a loved one in spirit wishes to say sorry for their actions on earth and desires forgiveness to progress and move on, and finds out they are not being forgiven. This is why it is very important to heal rifts and make amends in this life when you have the chance, if not you may suffer from guilt and deep regret when it's too late. I find this happens a lot and I see a great healing taking place right in front of me, when a family member in the spirit world tells their loved one on earth how deeply sorry they are for what they have caused. They are then able to begin to set things right from the spirit side of life.

Tragic Passings

From time to time, you will come across circumstances of unnatural deaths or tragic passings. Things like suicide, accidents, murders and early passing from illness, things you never expect to happen to your own loved ones, can happen in the blink of an eye. We all expect to live long lives, into our eighties or nineties, and so when a dear relative or friend passes at a young age or in a tragic way, the grieving involved can be harder to bear. There is a need to know that those who have lost their lives are safe and well in spirit and that they did not suffer. Parents whose children have died can be sure that their babies or little girls and boys are being gently looked after and surrounded with family members and angels who will take great care of them. The little ones will not be frightened and will be completely safe and secure and surrounded by other children to play with. They will meet up with you when you sleep deeply and your spirit leaves your body to visit the astral world. Your conscious self may remember some of this in your dreams but usually you will have no immediate memory on waking, although your higher self remembers everything.

When a loved one passes it is because at a soul level it was their time to go back home to spirit and this can be hard for the family members who are left behind. From the spirit side of life they want their family on earth to continue with their lives and make the most of it, as they are sad when you are sad. If you have the strength to move through your grief then you are making a positive decision to heal. You may be able to help others who are going through the same kind of grieving process, even by suggesting a medium to them when the time feels right. This is one of the quickest ways I find a person can begin to heal from the immense grief they are suffering. Anti-depressants and counselling have their ways to help a person grieving, but mediums can reach the painful emotions far quicker. I have had people who are sceptical and those whose religion has made them fear the use of mediums, come to see me because their inner pain of grieving far outweighs the chance that it isn't real or the control of a religion. Next follows a short real life story of how a mediumship message can begin the healing process of acceptance and letting go.

I Don't Want to Live Without Him

Many years ago in Swansea in Wales, I was working full time from an office as a professional psychic medium and healer. I had plenty of clientele and my days were full with different kinds of people from all walks of life, all coming with the same need of receiving psychic guidance or wanting to hear from loved ones in spirit.

I have read for those with relationship problems, financial problems and have also read for families involved with murder investigations and missing person's cases. One reading and client that has stayed with me to this day helped me to understand the importance of what mediumship can truly do. The lady in question – I shall call her Rose – came to my office for her appointment on time and in her own words, not knowing what to expect. I never know in advance any information of what they are hoping for and only know their name and contact number. I have no idea how the reading is going to go or if it will include psychic guidance or mediumship.

The woman sat down opposite me with her head hanging low, I didn't need to use my psychic vibes to tell me she was depressed. We made eye contact and the first words she said to me were that she wanted to die. I could see the sparkle and light within her eyes had dimmed and that she was just going through the motions in her daily life. Now you can imagine how nervous that made me feel, first of all, yes I am a psychic medium and healer and have studied hard and developed my senses over the years, gaining valuable experience to help others, but at that very moment I felt maybe she needed a different kind of help. My ego doubted whether I was qualified enough to help someone so desperately unhappy and I felt the pressure of knowing the responsibility of what comes out of my mouth could affect her state of mind.

I silently prayed to my guides and angels to help me and I felt reassured from them that I was able to do the job in hand. I now know without a doubt that the angels and guides of people who need help, gently guide them to the right person that may be able to help reach them in some way, through the right words spoken or something else that can help to kick start the healing process within them. No one can heal anyone else, only the person needing healing can heal themselves, but others can act like a switch to ignite the spark within again.

I gave Rose a gentle smile and explained the process of the reading but before I could finish my quick rundown, a male influence from the spirit world introduced himself to me clearly as "I am Michael." It was clearer than I usually hear spirit and so I said to the lady "I have a Michael here from spirit and he wants to talk with you". The lady's face changed and she looked quite shocked and now I had her full attention. I listened to Michael again who now told me that he was her husband. "He says he is your husband and that he had really bad pains in his stomach when he was alive". She nodded without speaking and her aura started to brighten and her eyes filled with tears. For the next half hour of her reading, her husband gave her the evidence that she needed to hear to prove to herself that he had survived death and was alive in the spirit world. Evidence like they owned an ice cream parlour together and the staff had recently placed a photo of him on the wall to honour his life and dedication to his business, how he knew that his wife accidentally set a place for him at the table for dinner and how upset she got when she realized her mistake. The husband told her how he knew she

94

wanted to end her life because she missed him and made sure she understood that their love would live on forever no matter the distance apart. He passed on personal messages of love for her and their children and by the end of the reading the lady looked at peace within herself.

Rose was able to accept and know that her husband was still around her and loved her dearly, although he had died. Her words to me that day that I will never forget were, "You do not realize what you have done for me today. I have been from doctor to doctor and nothing has made me feel any better, today is the first day I feel I can smile again".

This was a powerful message for me as I fully grasped the importance of how mediums can truly help those who grieve. I am honoured to do the work of spirit and help people along their life path for I am a healer at heart and the making of a great medium will need to fully understand the depth of despair that mediumship can heal.

We all eventually lose someone we love but some lose them sooner than they expect to. Honouring the grief process is essential by going through the wide range of emotions that come with death. The hard part is understanding and accepting that loved ones have gone in physical form and that they cannot touch, hug or see them anymore. Love never dies, only death of the physical body, the love will continue on, staying connected to each other no matter the distance apart. Letting go of the grieving is not forgetting the loved one, it is accepting and allowing the pain to release, helping the healing to start.

The Making of a Great Medium
To accomplish the work of a medium, there are a few things that you need to develop within yourself to be the best medium you can be. Compassion and empathy will help you with

understanding the grieving process along with using mediumship for the right reasons. Those who wish to be mediums so they can feel special and unique are letting their ego get in the way and will be in it for themselves and not for the highest good of all. Mediums like anyone else on this planet are also here to aid progression of their souls, just because they are able to communicate with the other side of life does not mean they are exempt from life lessons and pitfalls of the ego. If a medium is constantly praised for their work, this can lead a temporary blip in remembering their goal of being used as a channel for spirit and instead claim all the glory for themselves. I know of a few mediums like this but my lips are sealed. Following is a list of some important qualities that produce the making of a great medium.

Important Qualities of a Great Medium

- A compassionate, empathic person

  A heart centred and balanced person

- Someone who can detach from sorrow and the ego to deliver an accurate message

- Someone who understands karma and spiritual laws

- A person who is honest, sincere and is true to themselves and others

- Someone who respects their gift and uses it for the highest good

- Someone who strives to provide clear evidence of life after death

- Ongoing commitment to developing their mediumship by circle work and meditation

- Someone who is striving to progress their soul through service.

The Spirit World

Before you are ready to open up to the spirit word, it is wise to have knowledge and information on the spirit world and its inhabitants. This will help to release any inner fears of you communicating with spirits as well as protecting yourself from being spooked by wandering earthbound spirits. Fear is just a lack of understanding, the more knowledge you have, the better equipped you are to stay in control and deal with any issues that may come up.

The spirit world exists all around us in a different dimension to the one we are in called earth. When we think of heaven and hell we think in terms of up and down, heaven high up in the sky and hell down below us underground. This is only symbolic of different levels of dimensions or vibrations – higher and lower, the spirit world interpenetrates the earth plane and can go in every direction. It is our real home and this is where our spirit resides in between incarnations on earth or elsewhere. The spirit world is also known as heaven, and no matter what religion you belong to, we all end up going back to the place we came from when our physical body ceases to exist. Our vibes attract us to our own unique level of vibration earned by life experiences and knowledge and we are drawn by this vibration, to the place in spirit that matches it. This is known as the spiritual law of attraction and no one escapes it.

The Lower Spirit Realms

Those whose life on earth created misery through evil and vile actions will earn their place through their own deeds in the lower astral realms. Hell is a realm where dark souls or evil exist, these are the spirits that have turned their back on God and remain stuck through their evil deeds and refusal to make amends. They have the opportunity to see the light and make up for their evil actions but choose to ignore this and sometimes do not even believe that God exists. Heaven and hell are a state of consciousness as your vibration and beliefs take you there, if someone feels they will never be helped then this is what they create and can end up feeling lost forever. God has no intention of losing any souls and all are open to be helped back to the light. Even the darkest soul was created by God in its brightest form and through its own free will chose the way it created evil amongst others.

There is still light within the dark soul but extinguished so low that it is no longer noticed. God will send helpers like guides and angels to help the soul know it can escape its anguish and misery at any time. Free will still exists and the soul must choose to accept this help or not. Once accepted the soul is open to make amends for the evil they created on earth, this may take many lives to accomplish.

Earthbound spirits are those who, for whatever reasons have used their free will to prevent themselves from crossing over into the light, maybe for fear of retribution, and so remain earthbound and stuck in between dimensions. These spirits can wander the earth or choose certain hangouts like pubs or places of interest to them when alive. You will learn more about these spirits in the next chapter. A medium is sensitive enough to feel these spirits and can come across situations like this.

When you develop as a medium, you are opening yourself up to be able to sense, feel and communicate with spirits and not just during one to one readings or stage work. You may come across earthbound spirits who notice your light and vibration and will try and communicate with you. Earthbound spirits do not have to be dark souls, many do not know they have died and you as a medium can help these spirits to cross over to the light. You will be shown how to do this healing work in the next chapter on ghosts and hauntings. It is highly unlikely that you will ever come across evil kinds of spirits trying to communicate with you but forewarned is forearmed. First and foremost you always need to use discernment and if you feel uneasy during spirit communication then you need to end the link immediately. You are in control at all times and are able to stop the communication instantly by calling in your guides and angels to assist you or switching off by closing the chakras and grounding. Also your own state of heart and mind which control your rate of vibration can protect you by only attracting spirits to you of like-mind. Therefore a balanced and relaxed state of mind is always best for spirit communication. Never and I repeat never attempt to use mediumship if you have been drinking alcohol as you are then placing yourself in a vulnerable and unprotected situation. You may very well attract alcoholic earthbound spirits to you, unwise and unhealthy.

The Higher Spirit Realms

These are the realms that the majority of people on earth go to and are filled with more love and beauty than your heart can even imagine. Everything wonderful that exists on earth is within these realms but more intense in every possible way, along with other things you can not even begin to imagine. The spirit world is our real home and we have all been there before and our soul remembers and knows the true joy of life there. There are great halls of learning where you can study any subject in-depth that interests you and amazing libraries that hold more knowledge than you can begin to comprehend. There are music academies, art galleries, dance halls, every creative subject matter you know and more. Scientific studies exist there by great spirit minds to help bring medical breakthroughs on earth along with inventions of all kinds.

There are different dimensions or levels of planes in the spirit world, guides that are more spiritually evolved than us, exist on higher levels and angels and Archangels who are more advanced are on higher planes again. Those who are further along in their spiritual growth than us are able to mingle between dimensions and visit and help us to progress further along ours through their teachings and experience. Mediums can have guides such as Cherokee Indians, monks and nuns but also have other guides that may be just as advanced and show no earthly status in this way. Evolved guides are not concerned with focussing on themselves and are attracted to certain mediums, purely to bring spiritual teachings to our world. In this case you may receive a name and small amount of information from the guide and in some cases the medium allocates a chosen name to associate with their guide. Among the spirit world inhabitants are of course the animals and wildlife that exist harmoniously alongside everyone else and every pet you have ever loved and lost will be amongst them.

Through my guide and angel I am told that we each carry on our soul progression in the spirit realms and together with spirit teachers more evolved than ourselves, we plan our incarnations on earth or elsewhere. We are committed to experience different life themes and lessons and work on what service we will give to the world through our own individual gifts and talents. This is called our blueprint or birth chart and is what holds our destiny and purpose for our allotted time on earth. We are also given free will to make our own individual choices in how we choose to live our lives within our chosen path. God assigns an angel to each of us, to protect and help us along in our life and also we have access to guides and helpers. The helpers can even be family members who have passed on before you.

Soul Groups, Karma and Past Lives

Family, friends and loved ones on earth are with you for a reason, you arranged to have this life experience with them and have known them from the spirit world before you were born. These people are part of your soul group and you all help each other out, by offering individual or group lessons with the intention of soul growth. Sometimes you would have existed together in past lives and have reincarnated again because of karmic ties or bonds of love. Karma is a phrase that many people confuse for some kind of punishment or bad luck within their lives. Karma is basically the law of balance and responsibility, it makes sure that you are accountable for all of your deeds and what you give out, good vibes or bad vibes will return back to you. This means that no one judges you but you and no one so called punishes you but you. Whenever you do the right thing, helping out for the highest good of all or offering your services selflessly to another, you create good karma that in turn will help you to balance out any negative karma that you have incurred through your own actions in a past life carried forward or in your current life.

You are the only one who judges your soul's growth and because of the gift of free will you are able to test your own strengths and weaknesses throughout your life. Spiritual growth happens when you take the view of doing unto others as you would have others do unto you. If you have certain morals or expectations for treatment towards yourself and yet you do not treat others in the same way, then you are not living your spiritual self and also incurring karma along the way. Karmic ties from past lives can be because of many different reasons. If someone did an evil deed to another and they want to make amends and balance their karma, it does not mean they will need to be punished in the same way on earth. They can offer service to the person they wronged in a loving caring way through being a constant support for them in their current life, this will help to balance the karma between them. Two people can both do something unethical, one of them is spiritually aware that they are being unethical and the other one is none the wiser. Both will incur karma but the spiritually aware person will incur more. This is because they already know better and have ignored their spiritual truth. The more spiritually aware you are, the greater the responsibility you have, especially if you set an example to others.

Words of Wisdom

Now you have an understanding of the spirit world and its inhabitants, you are ready to begin a safe and controlled mediumship experiment. Mediumship is always an experiment and the medium cannot promise anyone that they will definitely make contact with the spirit the person wishes to hear from. Sometimes another spirit wants to communicate and the pitfalls of this are if the person wanting a message only wishes to hear from a certain loved one then they will discard the present spirit and message. To develop as a medium it is wise to be involved with circle work and this involves a weekly meeting where meditation and spiritual teachings are given under the direction of an advanced and qualified medium. To do this you need to seek out a place of study and there are many such places available like Spiritualist churches, Colleges of Psychic Study and schools or centres of metaphysical knowledge. Not only will you then be in a controlled and protected environment based on the fact that the medium is experienced but you will also have the other students with you to practice on. The key to strengthening your mediumship is practice and commitment and obviously the right intention of helping those in need. If you are experiencing any emotional distress within your life or have any fears, then you need to put your development on hold until you feel in a more balanced and calm state.

Let's take a look at protection and preparation.

Protection and Preparation

To begin this exercise you can ask a friend to act as your client as an experiment for you to try out your gift. Explain to them that the spirit who makes communication may not be who they expect and also ask them not to feed you with information and only validate a yes or no until the message is over and you can both talk it through. You are now ready to begin, again with visualization and imagination skills. It is time to open your chakras and tune into the spirit realm. You are also going to be working with Archangel Michael, the angel of protection, along with your own guide and angel who oversees the communicating process. I cannot stress the importance of using protection every single time you work as a medium.

Opening Up to Spirit

Ask that Archangel Michael now be with you as you use your mediumship for the highest good of your client. Ask the Archangel Michael to place a beautiful deep blue cloak of protection around you that will keep you safe from any curious or interfering spirits. Say a prayer and also ask your own angel and guide to assist you with your communication.

Now with intent, I want you to place your awareness onto and into your base chakra. Imagine and visualize this chakra opening up and spinning in a vibrant red coloured light, this chakra is now open. Next take the red light up to the sacral plexus chakra and see this chakra opening up and spinning in a vibrant orange coloured light, this chakra is now open. Next take the orange light up to the solar plexus chakra and see this chakra opening up and spinning in a vibrant sunshine yellow coloured light, this chakra is now open. Next take the yellow light up to the heart chakra and see this chakra opening up and spinning in a vibrant grass green coloured light, this chakra is now open. Take the green light up to the throat chakra and see this chakra opening up and spinning in a turquoise blue coloured light, this chakra is now open. Next take the turquoise blue light up to the third eye chakra and see this chakra opening up and spinning in a vibrant indigo coloured light, also imagine another eye between your eyebrows and visualize it opening up, see the eyelashes, lid and pupil. The opening of this chakra will help with clairvoyance, seeing the spirit communicator. Next take the indigo light up to the crown chakra and see this chakra opening up and spinning in a vibrant violet coloured light, this chakra is now open. Visualize a white light shooting out of your crown chakra, high up into the clouds and leave it there. Take the white light through all of your chakras, down your legs and through your feet, into the centre of the earth and ground to a chosen crystal.

You are now grounded between heaven and earth and ready to begin. Imagine you have a spirit waiting to communicate with you and remember you are able to talk back and ask questions as well as just receiving information. To begin the message flowing, silently ask or sense who is with you then follow the instructions below.

Communicating with Spirit

This is where the imagination comes to light and you may think you are making it all up because you are working with the mind. There are two types of mediumship mental and physical, mental is a mind to mind process and is what you will be using, physical mediumship involves the development of trance or transfiguration. Physical mediumship is best developed within a circle and under the guidance and protection of an experienced trance medium. Mental mediumship is what most mediums use when standing on stage or platform to deliver messages from spirit. Information can be so subtle that you may not even notice it if you are not paying attention. Just go with the flow and give what you get but below are a set list of what you would need to provide to give evidential information from spirit.

- Provide evidence of a spirit communicator – man, woman, child. This is you establishing your link with the spirit world.

- You can also go one step further if you have the information of who they are too the client, example – mum, dad, sibling, family or friend.

- Describe what they look like, are they tall, short, large or small, do they have any characteristics, hairstyle and distinctive dress sense, do they wear glasses?

- Explain how they passed; was it a heart attack, cancer, illness or a tragic passing? How old were they when they passed?

- Give the spirit's name or any important names that belong in the family.

- Give never forgotten memories that connect both spirit and loved together.

- Give any important dates or anniversaries.

- Finally, after giving enough evidence for the client to validate the spirit link, pass on any information the spirit may wish to impart. This can be advice of some kind, or they may just want to say a quick hello, sending their love.

- They may also be offering evidence that they have been around them lately by letting them know they are aware of what they have been up to.

- Next end the link by thanking the spirit and thanking the client.

Once you have validated your reading with your client, it is then time to close down and ground back to reality. Thank your angels and guides as well as Archangel Michael for looking after you and then imagine each chakra cleansing and closing from the crown down to the base. Flood yourself with white light and drop the grounding cord from your feet, taking away with it any absorbed energies. Make yourself a drink and something to eat if you still feel light headed to connect you back to the material world.

Understanding the Language of Spirit

To obtain the above information you would have used all of your psychic senses, clairvoyance, clairaudience and clairsentience, you may have also picked up on smells and tastes and should pass this on too if that is the case. Remember the spirit world will use your own life experiences, knowledge and memories to get you to interpret symbolical images or actual ones for what needs to be said. An example of this – my husband was in the armed forces and therefore if a spirit communicator was in the armed forces then my husband would have the same kind of memories and understanding as them, as like attracts like. He would then be able to offer wonderful evidence in this way because his memories, knowledge and information are evoked within the subconscious mind. Another medium can also pass on information in this way but if they have no prior knowledge or experience of what the armed forces entail, then the message would not be as vivid in detail as the other medium's. Think of it this way, how can you pass on information from spirit that you have no understanding or comprehension of. Most of the time a mental medium will use clairaudience and they either hear words form in their minds or have the knowledge transferred instantly telepathically from spirit. The spirit world knows if you are able to recognize the information or not, they know what they have to work with. Next are two examples to show you how this works.

The spirit communicator can only use what they have to work with within our full understanding and comprehension. If they place a word in our minds that we do not know or understand then we are likely to miss it completely or only have a feel for how the word may sound. The spirit world is very clever and they can find other ways to deliver information if the medium has no comprehension of what they wish to imply. An example of this happened to me on the rostrum when I was delivering a message to a Scottish lady in the congregation. I was being told about her grandson and his school work and the next minute I had a clairvoyant image of ducks on a pond. I gave what I got and told the lady I was being shown ducks. The Scottish lady implied that ducks was the term used for awards at school in Scotland and this was very significant. I did not have this knowledge within me and so they worked around it and found a way to get their message across.

This example is to let you know that you should always relay what you get from spirit and trust in the spirit world to supply you with the best possible way of placing the message. The next example is to show how giving names can be sometimes confusing due to the way our minds receive the information.

A man came to see me for a reading and his father came through from the spirit world showing me a boat. The man confirmed that his father owned a boat when alive and asked me if his father could give me the name of the boat so he could be sure that I was talking with his dad. I explained I could ask his dad and do my best but if it was a difficult name I may only get the initial or feel for the name. In my mind I silently asked his dad for the boat's name and I instantly received an image of the Royal Britannia, I knew this was obviously not the boat in question so I told the man it begins with the initial B and sounds like Britannia. The man nearly fell of his chair as he was in no doubt his father was now communicating with him, the boat was called Britannic. The process of receiving names can be likened to the predictive text on a mobile phone, you type in a word and it completes it for you but sometimes it is not the word you wanted to write. If the name doesn't arrive quickly enough or you are unable to recognize it then you can often attach your own interpretation to the end of the word. For instance if you hear the beginning of the word Chris then your mind can make that form into Christine but the name of the spirit is called Christopher. To become accurate with names is a skill that requires practice and patience and not all mediums are as strong as others in this category. John Edward is an amazing medium and great with names but he too also gives the initial of the name or the sound of it when he cannot grasp the correct meaning.

This goes to explain the myth where by five sensory people think that if mediums are real they should be able to provide full names, addresses and phone numbers from spirit. If someone wants blood from the medium for them to believe, then no matter what the medium comes up with, it will never be good enough and they will just waste their energy trying. A medium is not there for amusement or to try and convince anyone that there is life after death as this is interfering with the spiritual growth of another. The goal of a medium is to work in harmony with the spirit world and if someone has their mind opened to the fact that life after death exists then their work is being done unselfishly and for the highest good. If you are really interested in developing mediumship then the best piece of advice that I can give you and exactly what I did, is to watch as many different mediums work as possible. You will find they vary in strengths and accuracies but all are open to continued development through their commitment. You will notice the different ways in which they work and see how mediums that have strong personalities stand out and grab the attention of the audience more than others. If it is your desire to reach many people in this world through the spiritual work of mediumship then you will need to have explored, researched, developed and be constantly committed to the work of a medium.

Now you have an understanding of mediumship the spirit world and its inhabitants you are ready for the next chapter, to delve deeper into the mystery of ghosts, hauntings and things that go bump in the night.

Vibes Check List

- Psychics read auras around objects and people, mediums are channels for spirit communication.

- The purpose of a medium is to provide supporting evidence of life after death or what is known as eternal life.

- Another reason for mediumship is to help those who are grieving to kick start their healing by connecting with their loved one in spirit.

- The motive of a medium is a spiritual one and mediumship can also be used to bring spiritual teachings to the earth plane to serve humanity for the highest good.

- It is wise to heal any rifts or make amends in this life while you have the chance.

- Compassion, empathy and an understanding of the grieving process is the making of a great medium.

- Commitment and practice under the guidance of an experienced medium in circle work will help you to develop and unfold your gift.

- Never use alcohol or drugs when using mediumship as you place yourself in a vulnerable and unprotected state.

- Always prepare and protect yourself when opening up the chakras to communicate with the spirit world.

- Make sure you provide enough evidence from the spirit communicator from the set list given so they can be recognized by their loved one here.

- Finally be aware of how your mediumship is developing by recording your accuracies and also find time to watch how other mediums work.

CHAPTER SIX

Ghostly Vibes and Hauntings

You are well on your way to becoming a successful psychic if you have read the knowledge contained within each chapter and practiced the exercises associated. In this chapter, you are going to gain a deeper awareness and understanding of the paranormal. This is a very important part of psychic development and is often ignored because of fear of the unknown. Fear is just a lack of understanding about something and so by introducing knowledge on this subject the fear will dissolve.

Paranormal activity is that which cannot be explained by rational or scientific evidence and we are now going to explore the paranormal aspect of psychic development. The reasons why it is important to have a concept and good grasp of the paranormal are so that you know it when you come across it, and how you can deal with it, and the main reason is for protection.

Here I am going to explain all about ghosts, ghouls and things that go bump in the night as well as the darker side of evil spirits and possession. My husband and I have personally dealt with spirit attachment and clearing haunted houses of its ghostly inhabitants. Later in the chapter I will include a true story in the person's own words about the terrifying haunting at her home. You will also come across the term exorcism in this chapter which is extremely rare but can happen in unique circumstances.

Ghosts
Ghostly goings on happen all over the world and some ghost hunters claim to have caught real ghostly images on camera. Although this is fascinating, there is far more to it than trying to catch a glimpse of a ghost. First of all you need to understand

what a ghost actually is, as there are many different kinds of spirit activity.

Ghosts are residual energy and can be likened to tape recordings, an event caught in time and re-played over and over again, always in the same location.

A traumatic moment in time will leave its energy print (vibes) as an impression on the building or area, re-playing itself for eternity to those who are sensitive enough to the energy vibrations. You cannot communicate with these ghosts because they are just a picture in the ether and have no consciousness.

The reason they leave such an imprint in time is because the event was traumatic enough to create great emotion causing residual energy to form.

These ghostly imprints can be anything from 'soldiers' appearing in an area where a great battle commenced, to a beheaded figure floating down the hall of a castle. Obviously there are other situations where ghostly imprints have been left and maybe you know of a ghost story or two from the area you live in.

Remember that ghosts cannot hurt you because they do not exist – they have long since gone to the spirit world.

There are also anniversary ghosts and these appear as their name suggests, on the anniversary of its demise and tragic passing. These appear the same time every year catching a glimpse of the past, a piece of history in the making. What you need to remember is this, if you come across a ghost that does not communicate with you, then you can be sure it is residual energy left behind and not an actual spirit.

Earthbound Spirits

Actual spirits that can communicate with psychic mediums and who have not crossed over to the spirit world are called earthbound spirits. These earthbound spirits are still attached to the physical plane for a number of reasons that we will explore here, including the free will of the spirit to do as it pleases.

If we look at films that Hollywood has made to find an example of an earthbound spirit, the film called *Ghost* with Demi Moore and Patrick Swayze shows a good depiction of what an earthbound is. The character that Patrick Swayze plays called Sam is walking along the street with Molly Demi Moore's character when they are mugged, in the struggle Sam gets shot and falls to the ground in Molly's arms where he dies. Sam does not realize that he has died he carries on running after his mugger until he turns to look back at Molly, and sees her crying over someone in the road. Sam looks closer and sees that the person she is crying over is actually himself and he comes to the conclusion that he must be dead.

This is a shock for Sam because he feels alive and perceives himself to be alive although he notices that he is away from his physical body. As he comes to this conclusion the most beautiful light appears for him to enter to take him to the spirit world. Sam makes the decision with his free will not to enter the light as he is angry about his death and wants to stay with Molly. This decision has resulted in him becoming earthbound because he has unfinished business with the material world.

If you have not seen this film it is a great film to watch to help you understand more about the other side, millions of people across the world would have had their minds opened to the possibility of life after death through watching it.

So an earthbound spirit is a spirit that for whatever reason refuses to go into the light and back home to the spirit world or is unaware of the light. One reason being for becoming earthbound is that some spirits do not even know that they are dead. You are now surely wondering, how you can be dead and not know you are a ghost. When people die, in most cases they slip out of this dimension into the next dimension with such ease that it is like falling asleep and waking up again.

If the earthbound spirit has no belief system or expectation after death they may miss the light or the spiritual helpers that are there to guide them home and thus they become stuck between worlds. They become attached to the earth vibration without a physical body to exist in and so only psychic mediums may see or hear them along with other earthbounds of like mind. They are in a confused state as they know they are still alive as they experience this and so they do not believe they have died.

Some earthbound spirits cannot understand why others seem to be ignoring them and so they remain in a confused state unaware of the time lapse, they remain stuck between worlds. As there is no such thing as linear time once outside of the body, the earthbound spirit has no idea how long they have been in their sorry state and lose all sense of awareness. They may have been earthbound for one hundred years in earth time but it can feel like days or weeks to them in their confusion and they often repeat their days endlessly with no thought to changing things. Not all earthbound sprits are in this confused state – some actually enjoy roaming around and being nosey and know full well they have died but at the same time have no intention of crossing over into the light. A whole book can be written in this area and so it is quite impossible to cover all the different scenarios that earthbound spirits get up to. I will be writing a book on this subject in the near future.

Hauntings and Interference
Earthbound spirits can interfere with the material world and with us in a number of ways through learning how to manipulate energy. They do this by using electricity and by drawing energy from electrical storms and our own energy fields. They are then able to move objects, make noises, interfere with electrical appliances and generally do what they can to make their presence known. If you can imagine how frustrated an earthbound must feel through being stuck and unable to communicate in the usual

way, it becomes less unbelievable. They can be confused and also fearful and want to do anything they can to get our attention to prove that they are still alive.

People who do not understand this will confuse this situation with an angry ghost who seems to be interfering with their home and their lives. Compassion is needed for the earthbound spirit, they need someone to explain their situation to them and also to offer them the help they need to be able to enter the light and cross over. It is not in your best interest to share your home with an earthbound spirit no matter how nice a spirit they are because for the spirit to stay lively and exist in their dimension then they must absorb energy from a living source to sustain themselves. In other words you will be used as a source of energy and can be affected through sheer exhaustion and a lack of get up and go. So if you feel you are living with an earthbound spirit and you cannot find a reputable medium to help you there are certain things you can do to make it better for you both.

Now this is usually done by a medium and helpers and is called a rescue circle, but with the correct understanding of how to help, anyone can do a straightforward rescue. Just because you cannot hear or see the earthbound does not mean the earthbound cannot hear and see you. At the end of this chapter I will include an exercise on how to clear your house of ghostly or negative vibes and help an earthbound cross over.

The earthbound spirit will not necessarily hang out at their old home or around family members and loved ones as they can connect with other earthbounds who are likeminded. Sometimes enough time has lapsed whereby their family members have passed on and new people will have moved into their old home. This confuses the earthbound spirit as they have no concept of time and do not understand who these people are and they can be quite upset and angry even frightened by this invasion of privacy, they may then do what they can to get them to move out, and this is interpreted as a mild haunting. When things go bump in the night and electrical appliances keep breaking down or the television switches itself on and off by itself then these can be early warning signs of an earthbound spirit. Often light bulbs will constantly blow and need changing and the atmosphere in the home can become heavy through the sadness and low emotional state of the earthbound spirit. The temperature can drop, the phone can ring and no one will be on the line when you answer, objects can be moved and hidden away, basically the earthbound will do what it can to gain your attention.

If anything like this is happening in your home and you are too nervous or fearful to address the issue yourself, then a reputable medium will be able to help. They will be able to clear your home of the disturbances, getting rid of the heavy atmosphere, restoring it to its original state. They will also help the earthbound spirit to cross over to the light and into the spirit world, helping them and helping you to feel safe and calm again in your own home.

Poltergeists

Other kinds of earthbound spirits are known as poltergeists; this is the German word for noisy spirits. Scientific research is still continuing in this area but generally the poltergeist is known for being noisy and creating havoc in the home.

Research suggests that repressed emotions from a young person in the household may hold the key to any kind of phenomena outwardly manifesting and causing paranormal activity to happen. This is still being looked into but generally, young people are more in touch with the spirit world because they have not let the material world affect them in the ways adult do. They are more open and sensitive to energies and are more likely to be a natural psychic and medium. This can make them a target for the poltergeist to attach to their aura by the emotional charge that they emit, giving the spirit the energy to cause physical phenomena.

Again a rescue circle can be performed to let the spirit know it is dead and offer assistance to help it cross into the light. If the spirit already knows it is dead and refuses to leave because it is enjoying causing havoc, then a spirit clearance is held and the spirit will move on elsewhere or will be dealt with by the angels.

It is the free will of each spirit to enter the light or not and some spirits fear crossing over for a multitude of reasons and a big one being fear of judgement and punishment for any wrong doing or evil deeds committed on earth. They would rather roam around between worlds and remain earthbound just to be safe, instead of trusting in the light for fear of being tricked. The spirit may enjoy causing havoc because they are extremely bored and have nothing much to do. This does not mean they are evil though, just fearful and frustrated.

Evil Spirits and Possession

Now we get to the part where things become more chilling and belong to a smaller percentage of the roaming earthbound spirits. They have one thing in mind and that is to gain control of an easy target or weak willed person, so they can feel part of the material world again or to cause effect in the material world in some way for them to carry on with their evil deeds. Possession is the control of the will by a dark entity of which there are two kinds, one is an actual earthbound spirit who has not crossed over and may have been extremely evil on earth, for instance those who are violent or murders, abusers, manipulators and serial killers.

The other even darker, and what is known in theology as a demonic spirit, was not born as a human. One thing you need to know about evil, we all have within us dark and light energies or vibrations, we balance these energies and choose a predominant one, and anyone reading this book will be working with the light.

Those who ignore the light and choose to experience dark energies does not necessarily mean they are entirely evil as they have the opportunity to realize their mistakes and make amends by changing their focus and shifting their attention to the light.

Pure evil is that which has no conscience; it feels no love and has no intention of seeking the light within, as the light is so depleted to the point of being distinguished. The person is so far gone towards the dark side that it cannot remember who it really is anymore – originally created from the light – and their evil role is completely satisfying to them. This is a dangerous way to exist as the person is then opening themselves up to receiving demonic influences.

Demonic spirits that belong to the dark side wish to use these people to entice them over completely to their way of being, the more the better. They influence these people and get them to commit awful deeds through violence, murder and manipulation on the earth, they give them the power to create havoc and begin to take over their minds and will. Once they die they will either remain earthbound for fear of retribution and are used by the dark side to create as much misery as they can to try and entice others towards possession and demonic influence. Or they end up in the lower astral realms with other spirits of the same vibrations trapped in the miserable existence that they created themselves through their own free will. Unless they are willing to make amends, they will remain where they are, unable to harm anyone else.

The Dark Side

There is a dark side and their plan is to get to as many people as possible towards their way of being, destroying faith in people and their favourite is to get people to lose their faith in God. They look for anyone who has a weakness, especially those who have no belief in a higher power.

The dark side has no power over the light and will stay away from light workers who have strong faith and are completely balanced as they know they stand no chance. Bear in mind though, that light workers are also sensitive and may experience emotional problems and when they are low in spirit they can become targets to those who wish to meddle with their minds. If the light workers stay strong to their faith in God and remain balanced they will be able to protect themselves from negative energy, helping them to overcome their temporary problems. Sometimes this is a test to someone's faith and belief in the light.

People who are targets are those with unbalanced lives, people who abuse their bodies with drink, drugs, lack of sleep or anything that is out of moderation and placing pressure on the mind and outlook of the person. This lowers the person's vibes and therefore they become an easier target. The dark entity will have a very heavy slow ugly energy and will not be attracted to a fast light-hearted energy of a spiritual person with faith in the Divine. Spirits who are earthbound and who abused their bodies with alcohol when alive will be desperate to experience the same feeling of being drunk once again and they need to find a physical body to do this. Their aim is to gain control of the will and attach themselves to the aura of the person, influencing them to drink more alcohol or to take more drugs so they can feel the effects and get a kick out of it. They can then begin to gain greater influence of the person, so that without the necessary measures to stop these spirits, people can become victims of possession or haunting.

Exorcism

A medium can be used to help these earthbounds move over to the light as they are only spirit attachments and as the name suggests they attach themselves to the aura, they are easier to deal with then full blown possession.

If possession of the physical body has happened by an earthbound with no demonic influence then a medium will also be able to help to exorcise the spirit but if a stronger darker entity is in control of full blown demonic possession then a priest will need to be called in to perform an official rite of exorcism. My husband and I have dealt with helping those experiencing mild possession and spirit attachments and so far thank goodness we have not needed the help of a priest. This would be very serious and extremely dangerous if someone is unaware and unprepared to deal with it alone no matter how good a medium you are. I am pleased to say that it is extremely rare and you will most probably never come across this area in your life time.

At the end of this chapter I will show you how you can protect yourself from earthbound spirits and dark entities so you are not open to psychic attack.

Now I include a real life haunting in the person's own words.

A real haunting and spirit attachment, in the person's own words

'Since fireworks night on the 5th November 2006 our three bedroom end-of-terrace house in a small Scottish Royal Borough had become a house of horror for me and my young family. I had previously told my abusive husband that I wanted a divorce after years of mental and physical torture and was now living in my lovely small house with my two children and felt safe and happy for the first time in many years.

That very night our shower broke down and the dishwasher flooded, the bulb in the lobby blew and everything seemed to be breaking down. When I opened the door of the dishwasher a huge carving knife shot out flying towards me and I screamed, although it missed me. I thought I was going nuts.

The weirdest of all was that our placid dog who normally wouldn't say boo to a goose was growling at something we could not see. That night he lay across my bed as if to protect me and started growling through the night for no reason, and I felt really scared. Then my dog got really ill all of a sudden and he couldn't walk properly.

I started crying so I prayed to God to help my dog get better. Through the coming weeks the dogs health improved but the children started acting aggressively towards me and each other, life was becoming a nightmare when it should have been a great new start. My children started to have restless nights and had disturbed sleep and things started getting worse. The shower would not work even though a physical solution could not be found. A glass flew out of the cupboard at my face missed me and then smashed. I was not hurt, just in shock. Electrical problems plagued my house and my bulbs kept flickering on an off. The pictures along my wall were all moved and even when I placed them back the right way they moved again. The kitchen had an uneasy feeling and I felt someone was watching me.

The last straw was when I decided to take the dog for a walk after I had packed the children off to school. Off to the forest we went for our regular daily walk, when we had only been walking about five minutes, we came across a large tense dog with an aggressive stance attached by a lead held by his owner. The dog made a huge dash towards me with teeth gnashing and my poor dog hid between my legs in fear and dragged me and him into a ditch. I dislocated my fingers and cut my legs during the fall and felt sick with shock. The owner of the dog gave me a lift to the hospital.

My luck had never been so bad and I felt sure our house had something dark and sinister lurking in it that I couldn't explain. That night when I was home, my fingers started to swell up and had not been fixed back into place properly and so I asked the neighbours to look after the children and I drove to the hospital once again. On leaving the hospital with my fingers in a splint I was stopped by a police car and got given a ticket even though the police officer said he could see my dilemma.

"That's it," I thought. "I need help. Something is happening to me my children and my house and I want it to stop." My son had that day been swimming and jumped into the deep end knowing full well he could not swim and when asked why he did this after he was pulled out and rescued, he said he was made to do it. This now scared me very much as I feared my children getting hurt.

My cousin had enrolled on a psychic development course in Inverness and was really enjoying it. She told me all about Joanne Brocas and her husband who were the teachers. I had noticed them from an article I had previously read in the local newspaper and so I got their number and gave Joanne a ring. Joanne and her husband Jock agreed to come and check out my home and myself, to see if they could find anything paranormal. They like to investigate the problems first, because as they said, some people's imagination runs away with them and their fear can play tricks on them. I was pleased to meet with them and see that they were completely normal and lovely people who understood my fears and they made me feel safer. They checked out the house, going from room to room. Joanne did not like the energy in the kitchen area and said she sensed an earthbound spirit hanging around. Jock sensed a cold spot in the hallway and this was where the lights kept blowing.

They did a house clearance and gave me information on how to protect myself and asked me to see how things would transpire. What a difference, the house felt calmer and the children were less aggressive and things settled down for a while, but then seemed to get worse. Joanne and Jock came back and this time they made contact with the spirit that was haunting my home and attached to myself. They gave me enough proof for me to know who it was, and I must say I was not surprised at all. They held a spirit rescue and did a mini-exorcism on me and invited the angels in. Wow, what a difference it made, and my life is now back to normal. I feel safe in my own home again and I can feel a warmer lighter feeling that has come back into our house. I would like to take this opportunity to thank Joanne and Jock with all of my heart for unlocking the key to this ugly, oppressive and evil wardrobe and letting me out into God's light.'

This story shows how serious an interfering spirit attachment can be for the wellbeing and safety of a person and their home. Later in the chapter we will look at how to protect yourself from this sort of earthbound spirit's malevolence.

Psychiatric Hospitals

I was 21 years old when I started my own business running my own hairdressing salon in a psychiatric hospital in Swansea, cutting hair for the patients as well as the doctors, nurses and any visiting families. For two years, I came across all manner of patients with different types of mental illness. It was during this time of my life that I found myself becoming exhausted after every working day at the hospital. I can remember having a bath when I got home and not even having the energy to wash my hair, just lying there soaking in the suds. I was young and worked a typical nine-to-five job and should not have been this drained.

This I now know was because my energy was being drained by the low and negative energies lingering within the hospital. There were earthbound spirits hanging around, some were the previous patients who didn't leave on dying, on top of the heavy atmosphere of people's pain, confusion and misery.

All of this was draining the life force energy from my aura to feed the earthbound spirits and also lighten up the low energy. Some patients were in the hospital because they claimed to hear and see spirit people and of course the doctors refused to accept this as real and they were treated for a mental illness. This is extremely sad and it is my hope that one day psychiatrists may become more open minded and help the person to control their psychic senses rather than medicating them for being insane.

Psychic Attack

Because of my time spent working at the hospital it was a valuable lesson for me to understand how others' energies can have a huge impact on my own. I had not yet discovered how to protect myself and I was a target for anyone wishing to suck my life energy for their own. This is called psychic attack. Effects of being psychically attacked include extreme fatigue, depressive thoughts and irritability for no apparent reason, headaches or migraines, fever and sickness including rashes, lack of concentration, and not feeling one's self or out of sorts. You can have one, all or a number of these symptoms and you will find that if you have a headache or migraine then tablets are not able to shift it. You are more open to attack if you are tired, stressed and not grounded and then place yourself in an area of oppressive energy. This kind of energy will belong to very negative people as well as needy people or those who moan a lot and love having the attention off others to feed their energy levels. Negative people can leave you feeling irritable and angry and also give you headaches, needy people can leave you feeling fatigued and drained as they have sucked you dry.

You really need to keep an eye on how you feel to protect yourself daily. Remember you can do this by surrounding yourself with white light daily, and asking for the protection of your guardian angel but you must take responsibility to protect yourself. The more you develop your psychic vibes the more sensitive you become to energy vibes and so if you are not protected, you will feel it even more than others. Use your vibes as radar and as soon as you feel uncomfortable with a person or situation, make excuses and leave to detach from the situation or to prevent you from even going there in the first place. Your vibes and intuition can keep you safe from harm or danger so remember to trust them.

Exercise to Clear and Protect your Home and your Aura

You have to visualize or use your intent to see the most beautiful light from God around your physical body and aura. Then ask your angels and guides to protect you in the name of the light. You can use a sage smudge stick or incense but sage is far better, then light it and waft it around your body so that the smoke from the sage is clearing your chakras and aura. Then go around every corner of your home and waft the sage around, at the same time asking for the light of the Holy Spirit to enter your home. Make sure you de-clutter your corners and keep your place as tidy as possible. Bring light into darkened rooms or corners by using lighting or natural sunlight.

Include Sacramentals, pictures of angels or ornaments, a figure of Jesus Christ or any religious figure you believe and have faith in. You can also wear a cross and chain or have a cross in the house and other kinds of symbols.

Archangel Michael is the warrior angel and you can ask for his blessing and protection to be with you and felt in your home. If you decide to go on holiday you can ask this archangel to watch over your home and belongings while you are away, ask and it is done. Prayer is an amazing form of protection and saying the Lord's Prayer daily can help to create the light of protection within and around you. Pray for your loved ones family and friends too, as the power of prayer is mighty.

Crystals are also energizing and protective and you can keep amethyst in your living space or bedroom to uplift the energy. If you are feeling drained and feel that you may be under psychic attack then draw yourself a nice warm bath and put a small amount of sea salt in, as this draws out negative energy. You can also ask your guides and angels to remove any negative energy from you and to replace it with the light of God. Another thing you can do with the sea salt is to sprinkle it around your home at the entrance to doors and windows. To prevent any negative attachments or earthbound hauntings, stay away from the occult, Ouija boards and anything that you are not fully aware of as these can be very dangerous things to mess around with and can create a portal for dark entities to enter.

One last thing, remember that like attracts like and to stay balanced is to stay protected, so look after your physical, mental and emotional health and this will keep your vibes healthy and strong.

Exercise to Rescue an Earthbound Spirit

You can do this whether or not you can see or hear the spirit, all you need to know is that the spirit can see and hear you. First you would have carried out an investigation to gain evidence of a haunting or spirit attachment. On finding signs of the paranormal you can then ask for the assistance of your guide to help you with the rescue. Tell the earthbound spirit that you know they can hear you and that you desire to help them. Say you know that they seem to be in a confused state and that you understand this and will help them to know why, then gently explain to them that they have died and need to go to the light where there is only love. To do this, ask them to think of their loved ones who have died before them and to really focus on them. This will enable the spirit to see them again. Now tell the spirit to go with them and know that the loved ones will gently assist this spirit over to the light. It is as simple as that but you must do this in a kind and compassionate manner as the spirit can be frustrated and confused and may not want to trust you. A straight forward earthbound spirit rescue can be achieved in this way. Note that you must get the spirit to think of someone they truly love who has passed into the light and by their concentration alone will draw their loved ones near. There is one more thing that you can say out loud to an earthbound spirit if you feel this is not working, and that is to let them know that to find the light to cross over, they can attend another person's funeral. Most spirits attend their own funeral services and the light is there for them to enter when they are ready. Many earthbound spirits take this opportunity to cross over also.

You should be able to notice the atmosphere lighten and the temperature return to normal as well as any electrical problems in the house ease up or fix themselves. Hopefully this will have cleared the disturbances in the home and within a short space of time you will know if this has worked. If not you may need to keep a watch on the disturbances and if they worsen or become sinister then you need to call in a priest to deal with it or find those who deal with exorcism. A sign that things may be taking a turn for the worse can be a putrid horrid and overpowering smell that fills the house. Pray to be sent the help that you need, the power of the light will always prevail.

Vibes Check List

- Ghosts are residual energy, pictures and recordings that are caught in time and replay themselves out until the energy dissipates.

- Earthbound Spirits are those who have not crossed over for whatever their reasons and are stuck between the earth plane and the spirit world.

- Earthbound spirits interfere with electrical appliances and do what they can to make their presence known; some of them do not realize they have died.

- Possession is the control of the will by earthbound spirits or demonic entities.

- A healthy balanced life style along with faith in the divine and using white light will help to keep you safe and protected.

- Sage will help to clear the aura and house of negative vibrations.

- Compassion is needed to help an earthbound cross over as they may be in a confused state.

- Finally if you feel you have something sinister lurking in your home then contact professionals who are experienced in dealing with the problem.

CHAPTER SEVEN

Using your Vibes for Success

Now that you have a good grasp of energy vibes, I am going to show you ways in which you can use them to manipulate energy to flow in a positive direction. This will help to create success in making your deepest dreams and desires happen. This is called the art of manifesting and works through the spiritual law of attraction by aligning yourself with source energy.

One of my deepest dreams was to write my own psychic and spiritual books and get them published to be able to reach more people with my work. I have achieved my dream and I can only tell you, the immense joy my soul experienced when this became my reality. How did I do this? By choosing to follow my heart, the voice of the soul and by taking advantage of the synchronicities that came because of this.

I held belief in my dream and my capability to achieve it and finally had the patience to wait for it to happen, knowing all the time that it would. To literally live your life by following your heart's desires and choosing to experience what you really love to do, is one sure way in which you will start to attract to you, your inner dreams, goals and desires. I know that a positive state of mind with a healthy intent towards achieving what you want can help draw to you, a successful outcome.

In this chapter, I will help you to be able to start creating what you really and truly want. I will give you the exercises and knowledge that I myself have used in creating my deepest dreams and I know with all of my heart, that this has worked for me.

What I am about to tell you, is absolutely nothing new to your soul, who has been trying to get your attention, to consciously use the power of your vibes to attract what you want in your life. All knowledge is contained within you as you are a part of source energy and connected to unlimited wisdom, spiritual truths and total understanding. I am going to help you to remember the knowledge of manifesting success to bring it to the surface so you have the tools to achieve your deepest dreams.

The Power of Attraction

Everything wanted or unwanted is manifested into our lives through the power of attraction. You have heard of the term, 'like attracts like' and you attract in this way, through the resonance of your vibes. Every thought you have had will produce a positive or negative reaction that will ignite a feeling attached to the thought, giving it power. This power influences the flow of your energy and therefore your vibes are filled with the information needed to attract other vibes towards it, thus becoming your point of attraction. This implies that anything negative like worry over lack of finances will attract to you more worry and concern until you alter your state of mind.

Think right now, about anything that is in your present life experience that you do not want there, recognize the thoughts and emotions that you have in connection with the problem and start changing the way you feel about it. This will alter the flow of your vibes and the problem will eventually no longer affect you and may even disappear. Remember you can only attract to you what your vibrations offer, if you are constantly attracting bad situations into your life then you need to look to yourself to change the way you act, think and feel. You have also heard of the term 'cause and effect' or 'what goes around comes around', implying that the responsibility of your actions through the use of your free will, creates the world around you.

One quick step towards the art of manifesting success, to create your dreams and desires, is to become responsible with your free will, making wiser life choices. This makes you a conscious participator in manifesting desires into your life, as well as helping you to change and eliminate what you already have but do not want. Make sure that you keep a check on your emotions and not let them overwhelm you, plus anything that belongs to a negative vibe, needs to be altered through a reversal of thought. This will help you to retrain your mind and slowly but surely you will notice a brighter flow of energy in your life. If you are unhappy in your life, then you need to change your energy flow and yes this means you have to make an effort to do so. Do not let this put you off as the results far outweigh the effort needed to change. You cannot sit and wait for change to come if you are unwilling to change, as you will not help yourself to grow and learn. You already know from chapter one, that you cannot pretend to be happy when inside you feel sad. If you think you can trick the law of attraction then you are mistaken as the law is part of the most organized and creative intelligence that is allowing you to expand your consciousness.

Listen to your Soul

To be able to tap into the flow of the universe and connect with the synchronicities that help your dream manifest, you need to become true to yourself. This is for you to know and learn about what makes you truly happy, what inspires you and what makes your soul sing, thus getting to know yourself inside out. Then you will begin choosing to follow your heart instead of allowing fears to stop you. By doing this, you listen to the voice of the soul and follow your intuition, making you feel happier and fulfilled, doing what you really want to do. I am talking about the small things here that are a stepping stone to creating the bigger dreams and desires. Once you learn how to bring the smaller goals into your life, this will act as a sign to let you know that you are on your way to manifesting success.

Creative Potential

The power within the universe is filled with the most amazing, creative and ever- expanding source of unlimited abundance. This creative potential is there for anyone of us to tap into its source and draw from it. We do this through the power of our intentions to acquire what we want and desire. Every one of us has the exact same opportunities to be able to manifest what we need and want into our everyday lives. There is no such thing as luck, good or bad that can be used as a blame or excuse for why others are better off than you. The universe does not favour one person over another, it simply offers all of us the same chances and opportunities to grow and expand through one's own creations.

We all have the ability to make the best out of anything that we intend to do or be, to reach our highest potential that we hold for ourselves. Many people create their lives at an unconscious level and like a feather being blown in the wind, will have no control in where they are heading. They wait for things to happen, instead of participating in making things happen. My advice to them would be, stop waiting and start creating and this advice is what I teach every client who walks into my office. When you become an active participator in creating what you desire, you align with the energy of the universe and flow with it, not against it. This means you are presented with opportunities, miracles and synchronicities to assist you in achieving your desired dream.

Your soul is an individual portion of the most creative intelligence source and universal power, or what many people including myself, call God. Now read that again to fully grasp the understanding of the creative power that exists within you. You are a part of the Creator God, therefore your purpose on earth is to use this power to create unlimited potential, bringing expanse into your life and also to the lives of others. This means that what you create, not only serves a purpose for you but also for the rest of humanity to benefit from, should they desire to. The universe has unlimited potential to keep expanding and because of this you too have a clean palate to create your work of art. How do we create? You are already doing so, although, if you are not as successful as you desire to be or have not created your dreams and goals, then you are creating without applying the art of conscious manifesting. In other words, you are creating by default.

Vibrational Harmony

To achieve success, you need to align your vibes with the power of this creative energy so that you harmonize together and dance with the source of creation. Your vibrational energy will become in flow with the tune of the universe that will produce synchronistic results to help you unfold your intention (dream). Let me explain what happens when you tap into and flow with this creative power. By becoming a channel for this creative energy to flow through you, you are filled with inspiration to produce results. This means that the best work you accomplish is not created by your personality alone but with all of the ideas, wisdom and inspiration from this source energy. Great works have been produced in this way and manifested into our dimension. An important point you need to know to be able to accomplish what you want in life, is to know that you hold within you the same potential as any other successful person on this planet. This knowledge should inspire you to believe that you too can be successful.

My Story

My motto in life is to 'live your truth by following your heart' and I have always followed my heart in all areas of my life, especially with love. This puts you in a natural state of positive attraction, helping to bring your desires closer towards you.

I have always been prepared to take risks or change what I feel is not making me happy, even if I cannot guarantee the outcome will be any better. I figure, well if I am unhappy I need to listen to my vibes and do something about it and so I trust in myself and have faith in the process to make a new start. At times when I have listened to my vibes and made changes, because in my heart and soul I needed to, the beginning was emotionally painful but after the pain came the most immense sense of peace and happiness. One event stands out in my life whereby I listened to my soul and followed my heart even though to everyone else it seemed I was doing the wrong thing – and eventually it proved to be one of my best decisions that I made. The decision was when I decided to move from Wales to Scotland, leaving my family and friends behind. Everyone who knew me thought I was making a mistake and that I would be lonely, get fed up and be home by Christmas. My vibes gave me the feeling that this new adventure would be exactly what my soul would need to grow, learn and experience new people, places and surroundings. I was very lonely in the beginning and I missed my family and friends and nearly gave up by going back home. Instead I persisted in giving myself a chance to settle and make the best of my decision to stay. I decided that as I was going to stay, I would move nearer the city of Aberdeen as this would give me the opportunity to meet more people.

My life took off within the first week of moving and synchronistic events began to happen. I found a beautiful home on a farm where I had peace and quiet to work from home, I applied for a job in local health clinic where I could do my healing work one day a week, I got the job and soon became inundated with work.

The local journalist across the street from the clinic came for a psychic reading then did a story about me in the paper and this helped me get known for my psychic courses, healing treatments and readings. Another client who came for a Reiki treatment just happened to work for the local community magazine and through her I got a meeting that led to writing my own column. My client list grew and I decided to reach more people with my work by opening a spiritual and healing centre.

My life was flowing with a rhythm that I had not experienced before and I knew in my heart it was because I was listening to the voice of my soul and doing what I loved to do. When you do what you love, you are inspired to do more creative work and at the same time you become an inspiration for others to raise their vibes. An inspiring, creative person has a glow about them that appeals to others as a light and dynamic personality. They lift people's spirits by just being in their presence, inspiring confidence and change within. It is a good idea to surround yourself with inspiring people, especially when you have an inner dream that you really desire to make happen. This is because they uplift you and make you feel you have the courage and ability to achieve it.

During the next phase of my life I became president of the Centre of Spiritual Light, a healing centre giving demonstrations of mediumship, spiritual talks and healing sessions. I taught many students to believe in themselves, helping them to connect with their soul powers to serve them in their daily lives. I helped hundreds of clients with psychic guidance, giving them the help they needed to make wiser life choices. And it was on one of my psychic vibes development courses that I first met Jock, my soulmate, who went on to become my husband.

All of this happened because I listened to my soul and followed my heart. The point I am making here is, even though in the beginning I was lonely, had some doubts, and I nearly gave up, as soon as I let go and accepted change, then success, fulfilment and inner happiness flooded into my life. I have made some wonderful friends and I can honestly say that I was at my happiest I had ever been, up to that point in my life.

Because I stopped resisting the change I had made, I strengthened and raised my vibes and this created the magnetic pull to the vibes I needed to attract all those things towards me.

You can tell can when you are travelling along the right path, as life flows with ease, when this is consistent, all of your dreams and desires are being pulled towards you and because of this flow will surely manifest. Everything happens in the correct time, if you are impatient in wanting things to happen quicker, you will block the flow of energy and delay the unfolding of your dream. Surrender any impatience to manifest quicker and you will be back in the flow of the universe. Keep faith and believe in yourself and the dream you intend on manifesting, know it will happen and keep on keeping on. You will soon see results in your circumstances, to let you know you are halfway there.

Inspiration

From my experience of moving to Scotland, I learned to rely on myself to make my own decisions and I became more independent. I found that trusting my vibes and following my heart brought me deep satisfaction and happiness and this is what I passed on to others. My soul grew through serving others, teaching them spiritual truths and helping them to also feel the vibes. My spiritual teacher Gillian Sharpe inspired me to reach my highest potential and teach others what had been passed on to me. Because of this I have always strived to teach by inspiration, to inspire my students to believe in themselves and their vibes.

My intention is to bring out this inspiration in you, the reader and for you to, to be able to use this knowledge and wisdom to bring out the best in your life, as well as helping others along their path. This is a knock-on effect that will reach many people and bring love and light around the world. Through this selfless act, you actually attract more great things towards you, as this is the law of giving and receiving. If you give from the heart you will receive your hearts desires.

You have the Power Within

Know that you have the power within you to be able to feel the vibes and recognize if they need adjusting, this will help you to manifest success. A good intention to live by is this, if you can change something you do not like then change it, if you cannot change it, then accept it, by doing this you will stop resisting and creating stresses and strains in your vibes and life. As one spiritual teacher says, "If you change the way you look at things, then the things you look at will change". Alter your outlook and you will see and feel a new horizon to your current situation.

The spiritual law of attraction is the biggest key to creating your life on earth and making your dreams happen. I have given you the answers to naturally raise your vibes to flow with the abundant source of the universe and now you will learn how to specifically attract to you, what you wish for. To attract to us what we want we use the power of intention and this is how we let the universe know exactly what we want. When our intentions are clear and strong and are supported with the strength of our vibes, we are able to manifest our intention to make our dream a reality.

I will now include the steps that I took to create and manifest my dream as well as tips on how to manifest mainstream desires into reality. An important note here that will help you to manifest at a larger scale would be – to include the reasons why your intentions will benefit humanity. In other words, how can your manifested goal help to serve others? That is the secret to manifesting great things.

Seven Manifesting Tips

Tip One

Write down your intention and be clear what it is you really want and the reasons why you want it. You will have more chance of manifesting it, if your intention is something that you are passionate about. For instance, I am passionate about my psychic teaching, spiritual and healing work and have seen how many people have benefited from the help I have passed on. This inspired me to reach more people with my work. I knew I could help others through the written word and wanted to write a book, and this became my purpose.

Tip Two
When you have a purpose it feeds the soul and you become inspired to do whatever it takes to help your dream manifest. Now, as an example, I will carry on with the manifesting of my dream. My purpose was to write my book and so books became my absolute passion and reading was one of my pleasures in life. My life surrounded my passion and I lived, breathed and dreamed about what I would include in my book.

Tip Three
To break this down into actions, I lived my dream because I was already teaching students psychic development and so was gaining valuable experience. I breathed my dream through living my life with purpose and I began writing and recording any significant information and wisdom that I would include in my book. I dreamed my dream through meditation and visualization.

Tip Four
Daily I gave the universe my intention, through my mental pictures and imaginings of what I wanted to produce. I also prayed for the help I needed in bringing my book into the world. "Ask and it is given". I held this belief and had the faith that what I wanted would eventually happen and I did what I really needed to do: let it go and surrender.

Tip Five

The art of surrendering can be difficult if you set a time limit on it and are filled with disappointment if it does not happen. This can make you lose hope and belief that your dream will come about. Even when I got stressed and I let the element of doubt come into my consciousness, I refused to let it beat me, or give up on my dream. Instead I would pick myself up and had faith that it will happen for my highest good when the time is perfect. When this happens, you will receive signs from the universe in the forms of opportunities presenting themselves to assist you in the unfolding of your dream.

Tip Six

Use your psychic vibes and intuition to become aware of those gentle nudges off the universe and be willing to take the risks you need to achieve your desired goal. I followed my intuition and the universe provided me with the help I needed to get myself known so my work could reach more people. I got booked onto radio shows, television in Florida and got front page headline news with my psychic work, this helped me reach more people and at the same time gave me a huge sign that I was on my way to achieving my goal. Remember, you will know when you are on the right path, when you flow with the universe and not struggle against it.

Tip Seven

The unfolding of my dream – the day I knew that my dream of publishing my book was being made a reality, was one of the best days of my life. This was because it had been a deep desire inside of me to create this work and have my own book. Not only had I created my book, with the spiritual help and psychic guidance within it to help many people, but I had also achieved the one thing that this chapter is all about, 'Manifesting'. To me this proves that anyone is capable of creating their dreams and desires and that by using your vibes, the law of attraction and following your heart, will all add up, for you to achieve success.

Next are two exercises for you to use to help manifest your specific dreams into reality, creating the success you desire.

Exercise to Manifest Success

Prepare yourself with the tuning in exercise from the first chapter. Imagine and visualize a beautiful white light coming down towards you from high up in the sky and from the universe. This white light is gently falling like soft raindrops onto the top of your head and spilling over the sides of you into your auric bodies and to your feet. See the light filling you up from the top of your head to your toes, flowing through the soles of your feet, into the ground, and imagine it travelling to the centre of the earth. See it attached to a beautiful crystal grounding you to the earth plane. You are now grounded between heaven and earth. Now say a quick prayer something like this: "Dear guides and angels, please protect me as I use my psychic vibes and help me to understand what I receive. I ask this in the name of God, Amen".

You are then in a calm state of mind, protected and grounded ready to achieve your goal of manifesting. Now state your intention to your higher self, guide or angel about what it is you truly want to create. Take the next ten minutes to experience within your mind what it would actually feel like to be living the dream you wish to create. With emphasis on feeling, use your imagination and visualization to feel how happy and fulfilled you are by living your dream. Next you can look within your dream state for anything that gives you signs and clues for you to work towards in your present circumstances. An example of this would be focussing exactly on what makes you feel the most happy within your dream. You would then know the direction needed to work towards achieving your intention. Now use the power of your imagination to make your dream as vivid and emotional as possible. See, feel and hear exactly what you would do if you were living your dream now. Just before you come out of this dream state, affirm your success by stating gratitude for the accomplishment of your inner most desires, in a way where by it has already manifested. An example for you to use, would be something like this: I thank the universe for the success that is mine because I am a very successful person. Either use this affirmation or make your own to suit your dream but remember to always affirm you already have success.

Now you can finish and do the tuning out exercise and centre yourself by doing something physical, bringing you back into the material world.

Five Year Success List
Take your journal and write across the top of the page, the next five years of my life. Now everything that you would truly want to happen, your deepest dreams, desires and goals are to be included in a list under the heading. Even if you feel that you have no way of ever attaining your goals and dreams, thinking that you are just experiencing wishful thinking, continue to add what it is that really moves you within. Make sure that you only write down what it is that your heart and soul truly wants and not meaningless wishes. Now under the list, I want you to write a quick note, addressed to the universe stating that you now desire the help needed to manifest everything included within your list. State that you will use your intuition and psychic vibes to notice any signs and synchronicities presented in the forms of any opportunities to help along the achievement of your dreams. Sign and date the journal entry and know beyond a shadow of a doubt that you have now set the steps in motion needed to help you succeed in manifesting success into reality.

You should realize here that the universe knows far more about what you truly need to accomplish and should your dreams and goals not manifest in the way you intended, equal or better will given to you.

Affirmations

I will now give you some quick fix clues to flip switch any negative vibes into a positive flow. This is something you need to do every time you have negative thoughts and feelings. You have habits that need to be changed, by re-programming your conscious and subconscious mind to alter your rate of individual vibration and therefore point of attraction. This is a process that needs to be given a chance to work to see the results that you are affirming anew. Remember if you have been negatively thinking and feeling all of your life, you certainly need a few months to notice the power of the affirmations working within your life.

Negative money vibe: I don't have enough money to pay my bills and do what I really want to do. *Positive money vibe*: the universe supplies all of my needs and I have an unlimited source of abundance.

Negative relationship vibe: I am unlucky in love and never find anyone who loves me for me. *Positive relationship vibe*: I am worthy of love as I love myself. I attract love in my life with full acceptance of who I am.

Negative weight vibe: I want to lose loads of weight. I feel awful and hate the way I look. *Positive weight vibe*: I choose daily exercise and healthy eating and know what I need to do to become slimmer. I love and accept myself.

Now you have an understanding of how affirmations work, notice what areas of your life are experiencing problems and change any negative vibes into positive ones. If you constantly work at this you will soon notice results worth waiting for. The key is to focus on what you really want instead of what you don't want. You will then be able to place your full attention on what it is that can help you achieve your goals. Surround your self with inspiring thoughts written by great minds to help you believe anything is possible. Read stories of others who have found success to get their stance in how they became successful.

You know you are an eternal soul with soul powers and this gives the help you need that five sensory people lack. In the next chapter you will see what happened when I used my creative side and became inspired to gain information for the highest good of all. This draws to you the energy you need to shift into a state of high attraction and create a piece of work that can not only benefit yourself but all who come into contact with your work. This is the true flow of creative abundance.

Vibes Check List

- Stay in a positive state of mind

- Trust your vibes listen to your heart and soul daily

- Take responsibility for the use of your free will

- Reverse a negative emotion to alter it and retrain your mind pattern

- Keep a check on your emotions

- Remember you are a part of God and therefore have creative potential

- Believe in your dream, knowing it will come true

- Have patience that it will happen by letting it go, all the time knowing it will

CHAPTER EIGHT

Using your Vibes – The Conclusion

You have now reached the final chapter in becoming a successful psychic for yourself and to read for others should you so desire. In this chapter I help you to remember the fundamental knowledge and wisdom for you to use in putting it all together.

To sum up what a psychic is and does, as well as the spiritual influences and pathway that incorporate psychic development: you have already raised your vibes through receiving the knowledge and using the psychic practices within this book, now you will have this chapter to reflect back on anytime you feel the need for inspiration.

A true psychic, is a healer of souls, and helps the client to recognize and reconnect back to their soul's divine power. A psychic will use their vibes to help themselves or their clients to make wiser life choices in the present moment, therefore creating happier future experiences.

You have been given the information to help yourself manifest your dreams and goals into your life. You realize the power of living your truth and following your heart in helping you to raise your vibes naturally. You know how to protect yourself from unwanted energies, psychic attack, earthbounds and evil spirits. We have explored the use of mediumship in a controlled and safe manner, understanding the language of the senses. You know how to give an accurate psychic reading to others with the different exercises and knowledge you have learned. You have been given the awareness that you have a spiritual team of helpers to guide and protect you along your life's path.

This book will have given you the tools to help you recognize the power of your vibes to use in your everyday life. You have gained an understanding of vibes, the energy systems of the body 'the aura and chakras' including colour interpretations. Maybe you are also interested in the healing pathway after reading of the positive benefits in listening to your vibes. You now know how to trust your intuition and listen to your vibes to make the best decisions in your daily life. Intuitive flashes will help guide you towards finding the best opportunities for you to take action. Feeling the vibes daily will strengthen your personal safety instincts, steering you away from harm and alerting you to danger.

All that you have learned throughout this book will help you to see yourself as a successful psychic. Constant practice with the tools along with meditation will help to enhance and develop your senses to a standard that you will be satisfied with. This will lead you to create a successful life for yourself fulfilling your inner most desires. Remember to change your outside circumstances and the world around you, then you must first change how you feel on the inside. And that is the secret to creating success and harmony in your life.

I am now going to leave you with the story and reason that inspired me to write this book. What you are about to read, has already touched many souls, helping them to make important decisions and choices in their unhappy lives. It is by far the most important part of my healing work and I have witnessed the immense turn around in peoples lives through taking on-board the words spoken. I will tell you now, that I have given many people copies of this work and have lectured from conference podiums, spiritual churches and healing centres with these spiritual words of wisdom. There have been articles written on this part of my work and so these words that came from the spirit world, are spreading far and wide. The work is written in a simply put and easy style to touch the souls of all who read it. It basically sums up my passion to inspire others to use their spiritual gifts, to heal themselves and their lives. How do I do this? By helping them to use the powers of their soul, to feel the vibes so they can heal, they just need to remember who they really are; a spiritual being with a soul, living life on earth filled with the divine spark of God. I pray that you also take what you need from the words you are about to read. If and when you need them to help heal others, you will have the words to give them. Before you read the words, a small paragraph will lead you to why the words became written.

The Reason
Many clients, who come to me for psychic readings, wish to seek guidance and answers to life's dilemmas. Over time I began to notice that the fundamental issues most individuals were suffering from was that they knew nothing of personal responsibility or could understand little of their own soul's power. Most refused to take responsibility for changing the things that were causing them pain, moreover, they blamed outside influences or other people for the misery in their lives. They were blinded by their own ignorance and fear and lived in the hope, not belief that things would just work out for the best and more often than not, they never did. By sitting on the fence or the sidelines for instance, they waited, doing nothing. I wasted a lot of time and energy trying to explain to them that things would not change unless they participated in making them change and so I soon returned to spirit for answers – and this is what spirit had to say.

The Poem Changes
Our life is one of constant motion
Forever changing like the ocean
Fearing the outcomes we cannot see
We stay where we are and constantly be
We stay in the pain of an old romance
We stay in the pain of not taking that chance

We stay in our grief of a love that has passed
Not willing to move or let go of the past
We regret things we did or did not do
We hold onto anger and emotional blues
We blame other people and then ourselves
For the hurt and the upset and our poor health
When we feel we are ready for a new start
We gear ourselves up to play our part
But fear creeps in of 'what if I fail'?
I may be worse off than I am today
So maybe I will just sit on the fence
And wait till I get another chance
For staying no movement repeating the pain
Will just hold you back again and again
Remaining in pain not living your truth
Being stuck in your life being hurt and unsure
Not willing to change for fear of fear
Not willing to move or progress any nearer
Can cause so much sadness and other ills
Depression, headaches and emotional hills
Not knowing what's wrong is sometimes right
To ask yourself this **"am I happy in my life?"**
For if the answer is no, then aspire to change
What is holding you back, then spread your wings!
For freedom can come from the choices you make
The knowledge you learn the risks you take
When you make the first move you are starting to heal
Your mind and your soul and your body too
The spirit world applaud you through and through
Trust intuition no matter how hard
Know what you want have faith in God
There is nothing you cannot cope with, with God on your side
He sends in his angels who watch us with pride
For it takes courage to change and confidence too

Ask and receive the angelic guidance through
So the message here from the spirit world is
Go for your dream no matter how small
Do what you want go for that goal
Live your truth and follow your heart
Ask for assistance in order to start
Love your self and love your life
Because with love in your soul, you will never ever fail

This is a channelled poem, channelled by myself from my guides in the spirit world and received Christmas 2003. It has helped many people inspiring them to re-route their disorganized lives, to make changes that affect them and others around them in a positive way. The poem instils in us the divine guidance that is always available for us to use and the knowledge that we never suffer alone – God is always with us. God is always on hand watching us and has giving his angels' charge over us, as mentioned in the Bible. Our heavenly watchers are there for us in all that we require and all we have to do is to ask. Understanding you have this help will help you to overcome obstacles and adversities along your life's path.

Within the verses lie clues to hidden answers regarding our freewill and our own soul development – this allows change to be ever constant, bearing in mind that change is the only constant. We are spiritual beings having a unique human experience – in essence we are that divine spark of God. This means that we are also soul creators and we can co-create within our planned destiny, using our soul power of free will to enhance our lives. The poem also introduces us to the power of our psychic senses to trust and use in making positive changes. This brings spiritual freedom, a sense of self and a wonderful feeling of empowerment. Spirit intended these verses to become our awakening from a deep slumber allowing us to change and to change our lives in accordance with our destiny.

The poem enhances feelings of inspiration and desire for a happier more peaceful life. By making the changes we need, we begin to feel happier and stronger day by day, raising our vibes thus drawing positive opportunities to us. It helps us regain the trust in ourselves to make the changes we have so long wished for. We are able to forgive the past and let go of the hurt, freeing the present moment for us to feel peace of mind within our vibes.

When we truly learn to love ourselves we realize our full potential and bring our creative self into balance and flow. Finally, growing in spirituality we take responsibility for our lives and become a fully awakened, self-aware individual. This helps us to live our life by following our heart and soul becoming the inspiration ourselves to help others who are still spiritually sleeping.

The poem gives us the overall message of helping us to know that we hold the power within us to take control of our lives to manifest our dreams and goals.

The answer, love yourself and love your life because with love in your soul, you will never, ever fail.

It has been my greatest pleasure to bring this book too you, for the development of your psychic senses. Throughout the book you will have explored a spiritual theme that we are all connected through energy vibrations and are one and the same. Each one of us has a soul with soul powers to use to create success in our lives. Now that you have the knowledge and spiritual awareness, you will be able to use your psychic vibes to become the best and most successful psychic you desire to be.

It all happened in this way, because you decided to 'Feel the Vibes'.

God Bless you on your journey,

Joanne Brocas

To contact Joanne you can visit her website at
www.feelthevibes.org